INTERNAL OBJECTS
REVISITED

INTERNAL OBJECTS
REVISITED

Joseph Sandler & Anne-Marie Sandler

Foreword by

Otto F. Kernberg

INTERNATIONAL UNIVERSITIES PRESS, INC.
Madison   **Connecticut**

First published in 1998 by
H. Karnac (Books) Ltd.
58 Gloucester Road
London SW7 4QY

Library of Congress Cataloging-in-Publication Data

Sandler, Joseph.
 Internal objects revisited / Joseph Sandler & Anne-Marie Sandler ;
foreword by Otto F. Kernberg.
  p.   cm.
 Includes bibliographical references and index.
 ISBN 0-8236-2908-2 (hardcover)
 1. Object relations (Psychoanalysis) 2. Motivation (Psychology)
I. Sandler, Anne-Marie II. Title.
BF175.5.024S26 1998
150.19′5—dc21   98-34595
                                             CIP

Manufactured in the United States of America

To Patrick, Sarah, Rachel, Daniel, Ben, Miriam, and Zoë

CONTENTS

PREFACE

W hen we began our psychoanalytic training, the British Society was divided (as it still is) into three groups— the *A-group,* the *B-group,* and the *Middle group*—now known as the *Klein Group,* the *Contemporary Freudians* and the *Group of Independent Analysts.* The groups were held together by the "gentleman's agreement" made between the three women, Melanie Klein, Anna Freud, and Sylvia Payne, following the so-called "Controversial Discussions" of 1941–1945.[1] Life in the British Society has continued since that time to be marked by controversy, but this has not been altogether a bad thing, for it has forced some members of each group to sharpen their arguments so as to respond more effectively to the views with which they disagreed. Inevitably, of course, a certain amount of cross-fertilization has occurred, and we hope that not too many will regard this book as the illegitimate offspring of an unorthodox union.

For both theoretical and clinical reasons there has been longstanding preoccupation in the British Society with the topic of internal objects,* and it is clear that clarification of the concepts of internal objects and internal object relationships is required so that they can be more fruitfully integrated into contemporary psychoanalytic theory. Classical psychoanalysis confined the notion of internal object to the introjects, which were regarded as constituting the superego, described by Freud as occurring by about the age of five.

> At about that time an important change has taken place. A portion of the external world has, at least partially, been abandoned as an object and has instead, by identification, been taken into the ego and thus become an integral part of the internal world. This new psychical agency continues to carry on the functions which have hitherto been performed by the people [the abandoned objects] in the external world: it observes the ego, gives it orders, judges it and threatens it with punishments, exactly like the parents whose place it has taken. We call this agency the *super-ego* and are aware of it in its judicial functions as our *conscience*. It is a remarkable thing that the super-ego often displays a severity for which no model has been provided by the real parents, and moreover that it calls the ego to account not only for its deeds but equally for its thoughts and unexecuted intentions, of which the superego seems to have knowledge.²

Object relations were viewed in terms of the investment of an object (or its mental representation) with libidinal energy, or with aim-inhibited—that is, desexualized—libido; and the concept of internal object relations was not seriously entertained. Yet psychoanalysts are increasingly coming to think in terms of such internal relations and of their *externalization* as an important constituent of transference. Moreover, such externalization provides a close link between transference and countertransference.

We remember vividly how both Anna Freud and Melanie Klein unreservedly regarded countertransference as an impediment to analysis. One's own countertransference to a patient was not to be mentioned in public and had to be dealt with by self-analysis or a

---

*Hinshelwood has given a most interesting account of the frequent discussions in the British Society on the nature and function of internal objects in "The Elusive Concept of 'Internal Objects' (1934–1943): Its Role in The Formation of the Klein Group".

return to the analytic couch. Now, of course, the valuable aspects of countertransference reactions are widely recognized, and are not automatically dismissed as a sign of an unanalysed problem in the analyst; and the more is known about object relationships, the more can be understood of the interaction between patient and analyst. Over the past several decades there have been significant contributions to our knowledge of object relations and their development and internalization from Margaret Mahler, René Spitz, Ronald Fairbairn, Erik Erikson, Michael Balint, Donald Winnicott, Heinz Hartmann, Edith Jacobson, Heinz Kohut, John Bowlby, Harry Guntrip, Arnold Modell, Otto Kernberg, Wilfred Bion, and many others. More recently, there have been substantial and important contributions from the psychoanalytically orientated experimenters who have been studying infant behaviour—workers whose findings have been ably communicated to psychoanalysts by Louis Sander, Robert Emde, Daniel Stern, Joseph Lichtenberg, and many other workers in this field.

The ideas reported in this book represent a line of thought to which we have both contributed and which was brought to the surface in a collaboration that produced the papers from which these chapters are drawn, even though the papers were for the most part eventually written by one of us. While the chapters still retain much of the quality of the original papers on which they are based,* we nevertheless hope that the work we have put together

---

*Chapter 1 is based on J. Sandler, "Toward a Reconsideration of the Psychoanalytic Theory of Motivation", in A. Cooper, O. F. Kernberg & E. S. Person (Eds.), *Psychoanalysis: Toward the Second Century* (New Haven, CT: Yale University Press, 1989); Chapter 2 on J. Sandler, "Dreams, Unconscious Phantasies and 'Identity of Perception'", *International Review of Psycho-Analysis, 3* (1976): 33–42; Chapter 3 on J. Sandler, "Countertransference and Role-Responsiveness", *International Review of Psycho-Analysis, 3* (1976): 43–47; Chapter 4 on J. Sandler & A.-M. Sandler, "On the Development of Object Relationships and Affects", *International Journal of Psycho-Analysis, 59* (1978): 285–296; Chapter 5 on J. Sandler, "Character Traits and Object Relationships", *Psychoanalytic Quarterly, 50* (1981): 694–708; Chapter 6 on A.-M. Sandler, "Beyond Eight-month Anxiety", *International Journal of Psycho-Analysis, 58* (1977): 195–208; Chapter 7 on J. Sandler, "Comments on the Psychodynamics of Interaction", *Psychoanalytic Inquiry, 16* (1996): 88–95; Chapter 8 on J. Sandler, "Internal Objects and Internal Object Relationships", *Psychoanalytic Inquiry, 10* (1990): 163–181, and on "On Internal Object Relations", *Journal of the American Psychoanalytic Association, 38* (1990): 859–880.

into this book provides a theoretical basis for integrating a
theory of internal object relations into an ego-psychological—
or, more properly, a post-ego-psychological—frame of reference,
taking what is appropriate from our own clinical experience and
from object relational and Kleinian theory while trying to avoid
simplistic formulations.

The first chapter is somewhat different from those that follow.
It serves as an introduction in that it is a personal account by one of
us of attempts to come to grips with some essential problems in the
psychoanalytic theory of motivation and their implications for object relations. Its relevance for the remainder of the book is in the
provision of a basis for bridging the gap between the psychoanalytic theory of motivation and a theory of internal object relations.
In order to do this, we have emphasized the motivated interaction
between self- and object-representations in the unconscious wish
or wishful phantasy,* which can be regarded as a major motiva-

---

* Over time a number of different meanings have accrued to the term
"phantasy". It may refer to wish-fulfilling daydreams in the system *Preconscious* of Freud's topographical theory, but it may equally refer to phantasies
which were once either conscious or preconscious but which were regarded as
having been subsequently repressed into the *Unconscious*. Such phantasies in
the system *Unconscious* (the "dynamic" Unconscious) become, following repression, the content of instinctual wishes, as they are, strictly speaking, no
longer wish-fulfilments. In Kleinian usage, all unconscious mental content can
be regarded as unconscious phantasy. With regard to this latter usage, Susan
Isaacs, in clarifying the Kleinian view, wrote in 1948: "Phantasy is (in the first
instance) the mental corollary, the psychic representative, of instinct. There is
no impulse, no instinctual urge or response which is not experienced as unconscious phantasy. . . . A phantasy represents the particular content of the urges
or feelings (for example, wishes, fears, anxieties, triumphs, love or sorrow)
dominating the mind at the moment." Isaacs also considered mental mechanisms (such as defences) to be phantasies. This radical extension of the notion
of phantasy was quite different from Freud's formulation.

Although the spelling "phantasy" was introduced in order to distinguish
the Kleinian view of unconscious phantasy from daydreaming ("fantasy"),
"phantasy" is now generally used in Britain to include both conscious and
unconscious forms, although some authors retain the fantasy/phantasy distinction. In the United States the spelling "fantasy" tends to be used for both
forms. We have used the "ph" spelling throughout, indicating when we refer to
conscious daydreams and when to different varieties of unconscious phantasy.

tional unit in our view of psychoanalytic psychology. Linked with this is the conception, built on a formulation by Freud in *The Interpretation of Dreams* and developed in Chapters 2 and 3, that wish-fulfilment comes about through the gaining of an "identity of perception" rather than through energy "discharge". In Chapter 4 we extend the notion of "role responsiveness" and "role relationship" and trace the connection between the development of internal object relations and the regulation of feeling states. Chapter 5 presents a revision of the psychoanalytic theory of character traits, adding, we believe, a further dimension to their understanding. Many character traits can be considered to be techniques that the individual has unconsciously developed to evoke specific role responses in others. In this way an internal role relationship entering into an unconscious wish can be gratified by "actualizing" an unconscious wished-for relationship. Chapter 6, commencing with a consideration of "stranger anxiety", considers the important role of the continual dialogue in unconscious phantasy, both with the object and with one's own self, as a source of reassurance and "affirmation". In Chapter 7 the interaction between two people is considered in terms of their externalizations on each other.

In Chapter 8, the theory of internal objects as structured organizations is amplified and their clinical relevance discussed. The view of internal objects and internal object relationships put forward is that they are, on the one hand, essentially analytic *constructs* that can be used as a valuable part of psychoanalytic theory as well as for purposes of *construction* and *reconstruction* in the course of clinical analytic work. On the other hand, they can be conceived of as internal organizations (metaphorically described as internal objects and internal object relationships), which can be regarded as "templates", providing recurring themes in wishes, in phantasies, and in our interactions with others.

Throughout this book we have referred to internal object relations as constituted by self–object relationships or interactions of a particular sort. We want to emphasize that these interactions are not simply dyadic (i.e. as between self and an internal object), but can also be interactions between self and more than one object (e.g. self in relation to an internalized parental couple). While such more complex relations are not explored in this volume, the general principle of internal object relations as constituting dynamic "templates" for phantasies and other derivatives still applies.

Finally, we are indebted to Anna Ursula Dreher, Paolo Coen-Pirani, Marion Doyen, Mary Target, Rosina Perelberg, and Aurelia Ionescu for their careful reading of the draft manuscript of this book and for their many helpful suggestions. Elizabeth Bott Spillius also read an early draft of the work and made a number of useful suggestions from a Kleinian perspective. Cesare Sacerdoti was tolerant and highly supportive throughout, and Eric and Klara King patiently and skilfully transformed the manuscript into the printed word. Paula Barkay applied her organizational skills with her usual industry. Above all, we are grateful for the opportunity to have experienced the stimulating influence of our colleagues at the Anna Freud Centre (formerly the Hampstead Child Therapy Clinic) and in the British Psycho-Analytical Society. Acknowledgements are also due to the Editors of the Journals in which earlier versions of the chapters in this book appeared.

Joseph Sandler
Anne-Marie Sandler
London, May 1998

FOREWORD

Otto F. Kernberg

A significant shift has taken place in the last few decades in the way in which psychoanalytic theory has developed and in its application to psychoanalytic technique. This development has, in essence, consisted in the ascendance of object relations theory as an overall integrating frame of reference linking psychoanalytic metapsychology closer to the vicissitudes of the psychoanalytic process. This has facilitated the formulation of unconscious intrapsychic conflict in more clinically helpful ways than has the traditional frame of reference exclusively based on the conflict between drives and defensive operations. This shift in perspective emerged simultaneously within the British psychoanalytic approaches of Melanie Klein and Ronald Fairbairn, and the interpersonal or cultural psychoanalytic approach derived from Harry Stack Sullivan. This change occurred within the ego-psychological approach in the United States, under the influence of Erik Erikson, Edith Jacobson, and Margaret Mahler, and a parallel development occurred in the contemporary ego-psychological contributions of Joseph and Anne-Marie Sandler in Great Britain. Fundamental controversies persist between those who take up two very different positions. On the one hand there are those who believe that object relations theory and Freud's dual drive theory are incompatible—that is, those who adopt the interpersonal, intersubjective, and self-psychological approaches. On the other hand there are those who see drive theory and object relations theory as eminently compatible—that is, the Kleinian, Independent, and ego-psychological viewpoints. This compatibility also corresponds to my own view. This shift in the psychoanalytic theoretical frame represents a rapprochement between theoretical approaches in psychoanalysis which appeared to be strongly in conflict with each other twenty or thirty years ago.

The great interest of the Sandlers' approach resides in their careful and systematic elaboration of what might be called the various "building blocks" of a contemporary ego-psychological object relations theory, carefully exploring each area on its own merits before gradually linking them into an overall theoretical approach. Their contemporary ego-psychological object relations theory harmoniously integrates drive theory and object relations theory and does justice to recent findings and formulations regarding the vicissitudes of transference and countertransference interactions in the psychoanalytic situation, as well as with regard to what we know now about early infant development.

The present volume includes key contributions of Joseph and Anne-Marie Sandler in several of the constituent areas of this new integrating frame. They make the basic assumption that unconscious fantasy includes not simply derivatives of libidinal and aggressive drives, but specific wishes for gratifying relationships between the self and significant objects. Unconscious fantasy thus takes the form of wishes for specific relationships of the self, with objects represented by fantasized, desirable relations between self-representations and object-representations. The individual unconsciously attempts to fulfil these by bringing about relationships in reality, with real objects in the "here-and-now" that reflect a desired "identity of perception" with the fantasized and wished-for object relationship derived from the interaction between self and internal objects.

In this view, the expression of impulses and their derivatives is transformed into a desired interaction with an object, and the wishful fantasy includes the reaction of the object to the wishful action of the individual. Unconsciously, the individual sends out signals and expresses behaviour dedicated to the induction of complementary actions on the part of significant objects, at the same time being unconsciously attuned to the "role responsiveness" of such objects. These developments are particularly clear in the psychoanalytic situation, where transference developments reflect not only fantasized relations with the analyst, but unconscious efforts to induce in him or her complementary roles that correspond to "here-and-now" unconscious derivatives of the internal object relationship. If such roles are realized, unconscious wishes are fulfilled. The analyst's countertransference, co-determined by the patient's transference developments and by the unconscious role-responsiveness of the analyst, facilitates the actualization of unconsciously fantasized object relations in the transference. If the analyst is able to tolerate the activation of such a role-responsiveness and also able to contain and utilize it for the understanding of the unconscious wish-fulfilment implied in the transference, he may obtain a powerful tool for the interpretation of unconscious fantasy in the "here-and-now".

Sandler and Sandler go into great detail to describe the intrapsychic transformations in unconscious fantasy that lead from the earliest experiences in the mother–infant relationship to an internal world of desired and feared object relations that is gradually elaborated and transformed into an unconscious template representing self–object interaction. They describe the continuities and discontinuities between the most primitive realization of unconscious fantasy in hallucinatory wish-fulfilment and delusion formation, the complex layers of unconscious and conscious daydreaming, and the unconscious and conscious illusory transformation of the perception of present reality. The authors carefully differentiate between this conscious and unconscious experiential world, on the one hand, and the unconscious, non-experiential cognitive and perceptual substructures that facilitate these object relational developments, on the other. This clarifies, in a contemporary egopsychological theoretical frame, the differences between the ego as an "impersonal" set of sub-structures and the "representational world" constituted by representations of self and object, and of ideal self and ideal object. These are linked in wishful, affectively invested relations that reflect the gradual elaboration of drives, as well as other motivating forces, within the internal world of object relations.

Affectively invested and affect-driven internalized object relations are actualized in the transference not only in specific, fantasized desires and fears emerging in free association, but also—and significantly so—in the patient's character traits, particularly in pathological character traits that emerge as transference resistances, very often in the early stages of the analysis. These traits constitute the automatized manifestations of unconscious object relations and are activated as an expression of the unconscious desire to bring about a particular interaction with others—including the analyst—to induce a certain role-responsiveness in him. From this viewpoint, character defences, as well as the impulses and wishes against which they are directed or that they indirectly express, are, by the same token, actualizations of defensively activated object relations geared to avoid opposite, threatening, fantasized object relations. Thus internalized object relations—or, rather, the unconscious template into which they consolidate—are expressed in repetitive behaviour patterns that, in the course of psychoanalytic exploration, may be retranslated into fantasized object relations actualized in the transference and countertransference. The concept of role-responsiveness emerges as a crucial complement to projective identification as described within Kleinian theory, condensing the affects and behaviour unconsciously induced by the patient in the analyst with the analyst's unconscious disposition to resonate with that particular interaction.

In the course of this elaboration of the concept and functions of internal object relations, the Sandlers stress the central importance of affects as the link between self- and object-representation in any particular fantasized interaction between them. They highlight the search for safety in an optimal object relationship, a search that in some way replicates the original experiences of safety and the confirmation of expected role relationships based on the internalized infant–mother interaction—and they point to the role of anxiety as signalling the dissonance between the unconsciously expected and actual relation between the self and the object. In re-examining the psychoanalytic theory of motivation, the Sandlers illuminate the importance of the role of affects as motivators that may be aroused by drive impulses and drive derivatives, but equally may be stimulated from non-drive sources. What is actualized in the psychoanalytic process is an affectively invested, feared, and desired self–object relationship reflecting the unconscious conflicts embedded in the patient's internal world of object relations.

The rich and detailed description of aspects of this internal world contained in the present volume includes the clarification of the differences between the introjection of objects as internal structures, in contrast to identification as a modification of the self-representation by internalizing aspects of the object-representation into it. Sandler and Sandler describe the child's continuing reshaping of the self-representation as he progressively distinguishes reality from fantasy in his perceptions of mother and significant others; and they differentiate "construction"—that is, the interpretation of an unconscious object relation actualized in the "here-and-now" of the transference—from the "reconstruction" of past unconscious experiences. In this they stress the difference between actual past experiences, their internalization and elaboration by unconscious fantasy, their contribution to a template that reflects the organization of the internal world of object relations, and the actualization of the fantasies arising from this internal world in the transference–countertransference relationship.

Throughout this book there is a major focus on the interactional nature of the desired, wish-fulfilling object relationship, and on the way unconscious desires influence the actual behaviour of significant others. This approach, reflected in an emphasis on countertransference analysis, signifies a partial shift of a "one-person" psychology to a "two-person" psychology: I would suggest that the Sandlers in fact propose a coexistence of a "three-person" psychology in terms of their emphasis on the need for the analyst to tolerate the activation of his role-responsiveness in the countertransference, to be aware of the risk of partial actualizations of it, and to contain and use it as an "outside observer" to analyse the object relationship activated in the transference.

The authors have consistently highlighted the role of affects as a central feature of the activation of object relations in the transference. Their convincing theoretical and clinical illustrations of the motivational function of affects raise the question of the further theoretical step of considering affects as the concrete drive-derivatives embedded in internal object relations, and which, in that context, carry out the motivational functions of drives. In other words, in line with Joseph and Anne-Marie Sandler's formulations, I would raise the question of to what extent the concept of affects they propose—namely, affects as central subjective experiences (in contrast to the earlier psychoanalytic theory of affects as discharge products of the drives)—implies that drives always manifest themselves as libidinal or aggressive affects and their motivational force is always affective motivation. Anxiety, of course, may be the direct affective expression of the awareness of a danger that threatens libidinal relations, or of aggressive impulses projected onto a source of real or imaginary danger. And the affect of safety, which represents an aspect of libidinal relations (in contrast to sexual excitement as the most direct affective expression of libido) may be contrasted with the manifold expressions of unconscious and conscious hatred and envy, which are the dominant affects expressing the aggressive drive. From this viewpoint, the drive-derived motivational forces would always be expressed in wishful fantasies of affectively invested, desired, and threatening internal object relations.

Another major implication of the authors' theoretical formulations may be the consideration of ego, superego, and id as superstructures constituted by corresponding internal object relations, a point of view that has been strongly supported by Joseph Sandler's earlier analysis of superego structures as part of the Anna Freud Centre (formerly The Hampstead Clinic) Index Project, and his contributions to the clarification of the origin and functions of real and ideal representations of self and objects. One might conjecture that the id or the dynamic Unconscious might, in this connection, be seen as constituted by repressed or dissociated, intolerably desired and feared primitive object relations and their corresponding extreme and overwhelming libidinal and aggressive affects.

This volume illustrates the impressive creativity of its authors over the years and the seminal nature of their conclusions for the still evolving efforts to consolidate a contemporary psychoanalytic theory geared to cover the understanding and treatment of a broad spectrum of psychopathology. It is a confirmation of psychoanalysis as a basic psychological science.

CHAPTER ONE

On the psychoanalytic theory of motivation

Introduction

The topic of motivation is an extraordinarily difficult one to study and has preoccupied psychologists for many years. A major problem has been the fact that neither in the field of general psychology nor in the more specific area of psychoanalysis is there agreement on what a motive really is. Even when we turn to the relatively restricted area of psychoanalytic theory, we find that we cannot be sure whether the term "motive" refers to drives, drive derivatives, affects, feelings, needs, wishes, aims, intentions, reasons, or causes. This chapter approaches the issue of object relationships from the side of the psychoanalytic theory of motivation and is essentially an account of the development of some ideas that led to the views presented in this book.

* * *

Some time ago—in 1959, when working with Anna Freud at what is now The Anna Freud Centre—I had the opportunity to present a paper to the British Psycho-Analytical Society. The first part was a theoretical consideration of feelings of safety, and the second was a short account of some analytic work with a woman I had commenced treating some nine years previously, who had been my first control case. The theoretical part of my paper, later published as "The Background of Safety",[1] presented the view that

> the act of perception [can be regarded as] a very positive one, and not at all the passive reflection in the ego of stimulation arising from the sense-organs; . . . the act of perception is an act of ego-mastery through which the ego copes with excitation, that is with unorganized sense data, and is thus protected from being traumatically overwhelmed; . . . the successful act of perception is an act of integration which is accompanied by a definite *feeling of safety*—a feeling so much a part of us that we take it for granted as a background to our everyday experience; . . . this feeling of safety is more than a simple absence of discomfort or anxiety, but a very definite feeling quality within the ego; . . . we can further regard much of ordinary everyday behaviour as being a means of maintaining a minimum level of safety feeling; and . . . much normal behaviour as well as many clinical phenomena (such as certain types of psychotic behaviour and the addictions) can be more fully understood in terms of the ego's attempts to *preserve* this level of safety.

The feeling of safety or security was, I argued, something positive, a sort of ego-tone, and as a feeling it could become attached to the mental representations of all sorts of different ego activities. Because of this, it was possible to postulate the existence of safety signals, just as we have signals of anxiety. I suggested that the safety signals were related to such things as the awareness of being protected by the reassuring presence of the mother, and that we could see in this the operation of what could be called a *safety principle*.

> This would simply reflect the fact that the ego makes every effort to maintain a minimum level of safety feeling . . . through the development and control of integrative processes within the ego, foremost among these being perception. In this sense, perception can be said to be in the service of the safety principle. Familiar and constant things in the child's environ-

ment may therefore carry a special affective value for the child in that they are more easily perceived—colloquially we say that they are known, recognisable, or familiar to the child. The constant presence of familiar things makes it easier for the child to maintain its minimum level of safety feeling.

The second part of the paper described the case of a woman of 35 who had been referred for sexual difficulties—more specifically, for the symptom of vaginismus.[2] She was able to have what was regarded as a good analysis, as her sexual problems readily transferred themselves to the whole area of communication in the analysis. She had an obstinate though intermittent tendency to silence, and I commented that

> It soon became clear that this paralleled, on a psychological level, the physical symptom of vaginismus. The similarity between the two was striking, and it seemed as if she suffered an involuntary spasm of a mental sphincter. In time we could understand something of her inability to tolerate penetration of a mental or physical kind, and as the silence disappeared in the course of analysis, so there was an easing of her physical symptom. It became clear that she wished me to attack her, to make her speak and to force my interpretations upon her. She was able to recall how her sexual phantasies in childhood had been rape phantasies, and the thought of being raped . . . had been a very exciting one.

I noted at the time that a central feature of her personality was her intense masochism and a highly sexualized need for punishment. The analysis resulted in the disappearance of the vaginismus and a general lessening of the patient's need to inflict damage on herself.

Four years after we had stopped, I heard from my patient again. She was very anxious, as her husband, from whom she had separated, had been threatening suicide if she did not rejoin him. She started treatment again, and I saw her for a year. She did not have her vaginismus, but it transpired that she had another symptom—she was now mildly but noticeably deaf (having been diagnosed as suffering from nerve deafness). At the time I noted that it seemed "that this new symptom derived from the same unconscious processes that had led to her vaginal spasm". In spite of working through all the previous material again, her deafness persisted. However, an understanding of this came rather unexpectedly. I suddenly became aware that my need to talk loudly so that she could hear me also caused me to shout pedantically, as if to a naughty child. This realization led me to the understanding that

> ... by being deaf she could force me to shout at her as her grandmother had done when she was very small. It became clear that she was unconsciously recreating, in her relationship with me, an earlier relationship to the grandmother, who had been, in spite of her unkindness to and constant irritation with the patient, the most permanent and stable figure in [her] childhood. With the working through of feelings of loss of her grandmother, and her need to recreate her presence in many different ways, [her] hearing improved.

I took the position in this paper that my patient was not only obtaining masochistic gratification through her symptoms, but was defending against an intense fear of abandonment by recreating a feeling of the physical presence of the grandmother, "whose mode of contact with the child had been predominantly one of verbal criticism or of physical punishment". (We could now postulate that the transference reflected the externalization of an internal object relationship—or, as is discussed in later chapters, the *actualization of a wishful transference phantasy reflecting an internal self-object relationship*.) I added that "the pain and suffering was the price she paid for a bodily feeling of safety, for the reassurance that she would not undergo the miserable loneliness and separation that characterized her first year of life."

The week after I presented this paper, I received a letter, dated 1 March 1959, from Anna Freud. It was in reply to a short note of mine. She wrote—I must say, very sweetly—as follows

> Dear Dr. Sandler,
>
> It was very nice of you to write after the lecture. I really felt that I should write and excuse myself for not having taken part in the discussion. The explanation was that I did not feel quite in agreement with various points and I thought it would

Dear Dr. Sandler,

It was very nice of you to wait after the lecture. I really felt that I should write and excuse myself for not having taken part in the discussion. The explanation was that I did not feel quite in agreement with various points and I thought it would be much more profitable to discuss that in private than in front of the whole society.

Actually, I liked the first, namely the purely theoretical part of your paper very much. Your description of a background feeling of safety brought about by the correctness of perception was very convincing. It always reminded me very vividly of an experience with a former patient of mine, a severe alcoholic who lost of all control of reality and himself when drunk, or after a drunken bout. A psychiatrist in whose care he had been before

20, MARESFIELD GARDENS,
LONDON, N.W. 3.
. HAMPSTEAD 2002.

1. 3. 59.

analysis had taught him to recover control by
merely verbalising his perceptions of reality,
for example. "This is a table", "this is a stone
in the pavement", etc. He reported that this
had been a real help to him. I believe
many patients do similar things spontaneously
when under alcohol, drugs, or in fever
states: they test the correctness of their
perceptions for reassurance about their
own intactness. And, like all defences, this
can become greatly over-emphasized.

I felt quite differently when it came
to the second, clinical, part. I think
what your patient tried to re-activate
with the symptom of deafness was not
the familiar perception of the Grandmother's voice
but the familiar masochistic pleasure to
which she had become accustomed. There
seems to me a world of difference between
the mild, all-pervading, "functional" pleasure

of perception and a drive, an instinctive urge,
such as the one for passive, masochistic
experience. The latter is an id-urge and,
as such can set action in motion, the
former is nothing of the kind, i.e. does
not belong to the instinct world. To
minimise the difference between the two
concepts seemed to me a very dangerous step,
namely a step from our instinct-psychology
to an ego-psychology independent of the
drive-world.

I hope you do not mind my being
so outspoken about my objections. I bring
them up just because I liked the theoretical
part.

Yours sincerely

Anna Freud

be much more profitable to discuss that in private [rather] than in front of the whole Society.

Actually, I liked the first, namely the purely theoretical part of your paper very much. Your description of a background feeling of safety brought about by the correctness of perception was very convincing. It always reminded me very vividly of an experience with a former patient of mine, a severe alcoholic who lost all control of reality and himself when drunk, or after a drunken bout. A psychiatrist in whose care he had been before analysis had taught him to recover control by merely verbalizing his perceptions of reality, for example: "this is a table", "this is a stone in the pavement", etc. He reported that this had been a real help to him. I believe many patients do similar things spontaneously when under alcohol, drugs, or in fever states: they test the correctness of their perceptions for reassurance about their own intactness. And, like all defences, this can become greatly over-emphasized.

I felt quite differently when it came to the second, clinical, part. I think what your patient tried to re-activate with the symptom of deafness was not the familiar perception of the grandmother's voice but the familiar masochistic pleasure to which she had become accustomed. There seems to me a world of difference between the mild, all-pervading "functional" pleasure of perception and a drive, an instinctual urge, such as the one for passive, masochistic experience. The latter is an id-urge and, as such, can set action in motion; the former is nothing of the kind, that is, does not belong to the instinct world. To minimize the difference between the two concepts seemed to me a very dangerous step, namely a step from our instinct-psychology to an ego psychology independent of the drive-world.

I hope you do not mind me being so outspoken about my objections. I bring them up just because I liked the theoretical part.

Yours sincerely,

Anna Freud

Anna Freud was, of course, quite correct in her view that the pleasures associated with direct instinctual gratification have a quality that is markedly different from what she called "mild all-pervading 'functional' pleasure". Without doubt, her major concern was, as she put it, to prevent what she saw as the dangerous step "from our instinctual psychology to an ego psychology independent of the drive world". I think that we can understand this very well in view of the need of psychoanalysis, throughout its history, to protect its basic notions from those who wished to minimize the importance of infantile sexual and aggressive drives, and the role of persisting instinctual impulses of this sort in adult life.

I must confess that although I felt abashed by Anna Freud's comments, a niggling feeling remained that neither of us had really come to grips with the problems involved in the disagreement between us, and it is only many years later that I found myself able to be more precise about where these problems lie. In what follows I shall attempt to work my way towards a suitable response to Anna Freud's comments and shall do this by a less than direct route.

In the following year, under the influence of writers such as Edith Jacobson, Edward Bibring, and Annie Reich, I found myself referring, in a paper "On the Concept of Superego",[3] not only to feelings of safety, but also to feelings of well-being and self-esteem. It was possible to comment, for example, on the topic of identification as follows:

> If we recall the joy with which the very young child imitates, consciously or unconsciously, a parent or an older sibling, we can see that identification represents an important technique by which the child feels loved and obtains an inner state of well-being. We might say that [through identification] the esteem in which the omnipotent and admired object is held is duplicated in the self and increases self-esteem. The child feels at one with the object and close to it, and temporarily regains the "good" feelings that he experienced during the earliest days of life. Identificatory behaviour is further reinforced by the love, approval, and praise of the real object, and it is quite striking to observe the extent to which the education of the child progresses through the reward, not only of feeling omnipotent like the idealized parent, but also through the very positive signs of love and approval granted by parents and educators to the child. The sources of "feeling loved", and

of self-esteem, are the real figures in the child's environment; and in these first years identificatory behaviour is directed by the child toward enhancing, via these real figures, his feeling of inner well-being.

I went on to suggest that the same feelings can be obtained through compliance with the precepts of the superego introject or by identification with that introject, and I wrote that, in contrast to unpleasant feelings such as guilt and unworthiness, an

> *opposite* and equally important affective state is also experienced by the ego, a state which occurs when the ego and superego are functioning together in a smooth and harmonious fashion; that is, when the feeling of being loved is restored by the approval of the superego. Perhaps this is best described as a state of mental comfort and well-being. . . . It is the counterpart of the affect experienced by the child when his parents show signs of approval and pleasure at his performance, when the earliest state of being at one with his mother is temporarily regained. It is related to the affective background of self-confidence and self-assurance. . . . There has been a strong tendency in psychoanalytic writing to overlook the very positive side of the child's relationship to his superego; a relation based on the fact that it can also be a splendid source of love and well-being. It functions to approve as well as to disapprove.

On looking back at that paper, it now seems clear to me that I was struggling to deal with a conflict over my deep conviction that psychoanalytic theory had to take account of other strong motives that were not instinctual drive impulses—in particular, the need to experience or control feeling states of one sort or another. I was, I think, beginning to be involved in much the same sort of problem that concerned many others. At that time my way of dealing with the issue was to do what was perhaps commonly done—that is, to follow Freud in making use of his own solution to this theoretical conflict by shifting the emphasis from the drive impulse itself to the hypothetical energies regarded as derived from the drives and making the assumption that such energies entered into all motives. So I wrote, for example, that in identification with another person "some of the libidinal cathexis of the object is transferred to the self"; but in a footnote to the paper I commented:

The problem of what it means to "feel loved", or to "restore narcissistic cathexis", is one that has as yet been insufficiently explored. What the child is attempting to restore is an affective state of well-being which we can correlate, in terms of energy, with the level of narcissistic cathexis of the self.

Having said this, I was able to put drive energies to one side and to talk again about feeling states:

> Initially this affective state, which normally forms a background to everyday experience, must be the state of bodily well-being which the infant experiences when his instinctual needs have been satisfied (as distinct from the pleasure in their satisfaction). This affective state later becomes localized in the self, and we see aspects of it in feelings of self-esteem as well as in normal background feelings of safety. . . . The maintenance of this *central affective state* is perhaps the most powerful motive for ego development, and we must regard the young child (and later the adult) as seeking well-being as well as pleasure seeking; the two are by no means the same, and in analysis we can often observe a conflict between the two.

The connection between the state of well-being and libido distribution was reiterated—now with more manifestly mixed feelings—in a 1962 paper on "Psychology and Psychoanalysis".[4] But an increasing emphasis was also placed on the child's object relationships.

> From a psychological point of view it makes a great deal of sense to speak of the child's feeling of well-being as located in his self representation, when a particular representational relationship exists between the self and mother representations. We can then link the state of the child's libido with the particular relationship of the two images at the time—those of himself and of the loving parent.

This theme was reflected in a paper published almost simultaneously with B. Rosenblatt on "The Concept of the Representational World",[5] in which, among other things, feelings of well-being were linked—I would now say simply through force of habit and quite unnecessarily—with the notion of the narcissistic libidinal cathexis of the self-representation. The following year, two colleagues and I discussed the idea of the ideal self (not the "idealized self") in a paper on "The Ego Ideal and the Ideal Self".[6] There we said that

> One of the shapes which the self representation can assume is that which we can call the *ideal self*, that is, that which, at any moment, is a desired shape of the self—the "self-I-want-to-be". This is that shape of the self which, at that particular time, in those circumstances, and under the influence of the particular instinctual impulse of the moment, is the shape which would yield the greatest degree of well-being for the child. It is the shape which would provide the highest degree of narcissistic gratification and would minimize the quantity of aggressive discharge on the self. The ideal self at any moment is not necessarily simply that shape of the self which represents instinctual impulses as being fulfilled but will be determined as well by the child's need to gain the love and approval of his parents or introjects, or to avoid their disapproval.

It will be clear by now that the states of safety and well-being considered in all these papers must be intimately connected with the problem of motivation, although it was not explicitly referred to. A motivational statement is implicit, for example, in such remarks as

> the construction of an ideal self, and the efforts to attain it, constitute an attempt to restore, sometimes in a most roundabout way, the primary narcissistic state of the earliest weeks of life. But the effort to attain the ideal self is not always successful. If the individual cannot change the shape of his self so as to identify it with his ideal self, then he will suffer the pangs of disappointment and the affective states associated with lowered self-esteem.

This statement contains references to two sets of motivating forces. In the first place there is the attraction of the ideal self, of the set of good feelings that accompanies identification with one's own ideal of the moment. Secondly, there is also the motivating power of the feelings that accompany the discrepancy between the representation of the so-called actual self—the "self-of-the-moment"—and the representation of the ideal self at that moment. I should mention that the notion of an ideal self was to be expanded soon after this into that of the "ideal state", for the wished-for state of affairs at any given time may involve more than a representation of the self, as in the representation of a wished-for self–object interaction. So the presence of an ideal object may be as much a part of the ideal state as the ideal self. The emphasis on object relationships was increasing, while at the same time the strain of bringing the energy theory into the picture in order to reduce motivation to drives and drive-derivatives was becoming too great.

In 1964 W. G. Joffe and I presented a paper, "On Skill and Sublimation",[7] suggesting that sublimation might be better dealt with by "a theory of displacement and affect change rather than [by] one of energy transformation". We commented:

> The fact that the functioning of the ego apparatuses yields pleasurable feelings means that we have a whole hierarchy of affective feeling tones within the ego, associated with the hierarchy of ego functions and apparatuses. These range from crude sensual experiences to feelings of safety and well-being and the more subtle feelings which Hartmann has called "positive value accents"... the component which differentiates constant object relationships from id-satisfying ones is a contribution of the ego, an additional affective ego value cathexis that we could describe in such terms as "non sensual love", "esteem for the object" etc. This is not the same as the aim-inhibited instinctual components.

Now, however, there was more specific reference to "motive forces" and to what was called ego motivation. We said:

> We have suggested that there is a hierarchy of positive feelings that the ego is capable of experiencing. Similarly we could postulate a hierarchy of "unpleasures" of all gradations. If we take the view that the ego functions to maintain a positive feeling of well-being in the self, then the experiencing of any degree of unpleasure will set in motion the adaptive and defensive function of the ego apparatuses. This homeostatic view enables us to consider the dynamics of independent ego functioning in the light of motive forces associated with the various ego apparatuses, which have as their aim the avoidance of unpleasure and preservation of well-being. We can in this way contain a theory of ego motivation within a structural framework. These motive forces can be

seen as "demands for work" (similar to that imposed by the drives) on the ego apparatuses. This "demand for work" is again quite different from the energy that "powers" the apparatus.

In the year following the presentation of this paper, in two papers on depression in childhood,[8] we made extensive use of the idea of pain as a motivating factor in mental life: pain as an affective state, or as a potential state that could be defended against. Pain was connected with a discrepancy between what we called the actual (or current) state of the self on the one hand, and an ideal state of well-being on the other. We said:

> Ideal in this context refers to a state of well-being, a state which is fundamentally affective and which normally accompanies the harmonious and integrated functioning of all the biological and mental structures. . . . The striving towards the attainment of an ideal state is basic in human development and functioning. It represents the feeling component which is attributed to the state of primary narcissism.[9] Much of the dynamics of ego functioning can be understood in terms of the ego's striving to maintain or attain a state of well-being; a state which even in the child who has been unhappy from birth, exists as a biological goal. Freud put it: "The development of the ego consists in a departure from primary narcissism and gives rise to a vigorous attempt to recover that state." The ideal state of well-being is closely linked with feelings of safety and security. It is the polar opposite of feelings of pain, anxiety or discomfort, and bears the same relation to these as the state of bodily satiation and contentment in a small infant bears to the unpleasure of instinctual tension. The attainment of this state may follow or accompany successful drive-discharge, but there are circumstances in which drive-satisfaction does not lead to the development of well-being, but to the experiencing of its opposite, as in states of mental conflict.
>
> In this there is a qualitative difference between the systems id and ego. The drives are characterized by states of tension and demands for discharge (and the body-pleasures associated with such discharge) which change in the course of development. The dynamics of ego functioning appear to be much more related to the maintenance of affective states of

well-being which do not change as grossly in the course of development (although the ideational content associated with the ideal state may change markedly) . . . we shall use the term ideal state to refer to the affective state of well-being, and the term ideal self to denote the particular shape of the self-representation at any moment in the individual's life which is believed, consciously or unconsciously, to embody the ideal state. As the representational world of the child becomes increasingly structured, his system of self-representations includes images which reflect affective states of well-being. The "ideal self" derives its content not only from affect representations, but also contains ideational components which originate from various sources. These sources include memories of actual states of well-being previously experienced, or of fantastic or symbolic elaborations of such states. The elaboration in phantasy may subserve defensive functions, in which case we may get magical and omnipotent components in the ideal self. The specialized form of ideal which ensues when the child needs to aggrandize himself for the purpose of defence can be referred to as the "idealized self", but it should be borne in mind that idealization is only one possible source of the content of the ideal self. Similarly, where the ideal self is based on identifications with an admired object, we can distinguish between qualities which the child attributes to the object because of its infantile perception of the object at the time, and those which are attributed to the object representation in phantasy.[10]

The relation to the object was seen as of crucial importance in the attainment and maintenance of an ideal state. We said:

> Object love, like the whole development of the ego, can be seen as a roundabout way of attempting to restore the ideal primary narcissistic state. The perception of the presence of the love object when its presence is expected is, moreover, a source of feelings of well-being and safety. This is true even when the object is fulfilling no drive-reducing role.

What is crucial is not only the presence of the object, but also the repeated experience of a satisfactory *interaction* with the object in reality or in phantasy (see Chapter 4).

It is clear that if the presence of the object is a condition for a state of well-being in the self, then loss of the object signifies the loss of an aspect of the self, of a state of the self. One might say that for the representation of every love object there is a part of the self representation which is complementary to it, that is, the part which *reflects the relationship to the object*, and which constitutes the link between self and object. We can refer to this as the object-complementary aspect of the self representation.

An attempt in 1967 to look more closely at the theory of narcissism included an extensive discussion of the relation of affects to the energy theory, and it was remarked there that

> from the moment the infant becomes a psychological being, from the moment it begins to construct a representational world as the mediator of adaptation, much of its functioning is regulated by feeling states of one sort or another. The demands of the drives, and the reduction of these demands, have a major influence on feeling states, *but they are not the only influence*. Feeling states are produced and influenced by stimuli arising from sources other than the drives, for example, from the external environment; and *it is an oversimplification to assume that the vicissitudes of the development of affects are a direct reflection of the vicissitudes of the drives*.[11]

We went on to say:

> Freud drew attention to the function of the affect of anxiety as a signal which initiates special forms of adaptive activity,[12] and we believe that there is a strong argument in favour of the idea that all adaptive activity, defensive or otherwise, is instigated and regulated by the ego's conscious and unconscious scanning and perception of changes in its feeling states ... during the course of development affective experiences become increasingly integrated with ideational content, and aspects of both self and object representations become linked with affective qualities, often of the most complicated sort. In this connection, the notion of an *affective cathexis* of a representation becomes meaningful and valuable; and affective cathexes can range from the most primitive feelings of pleasure and unpleasure to the subtle complexities of love and hate.

We then gave a definition of narcissistic disorder related to the need to deal with a latent threatening state of pain and to restore well-being by particular sorts of defensive and adaptive manoeuvres. Perhaps of interest in the present context is the re-introduction of the idea of a cathexis of *value*, mentioned in our previous paper on sublimation. We said:

> By "value" . . . we do not refer specifically to moral value, but the term is used rather in the sense of feeling qualities which may be positive or negative, relatively simple or extremely complicated. It is these affective values, sign-values so to speak, which give all representations their significance to the ego.

The line of thought we were pursuing was continued in a paper on the psychoanalytic psychology of adaptation in the following year, in which we commented as follows:

> Although thus far we have spoken of the discrepancy between actual and ideal states of the self-representation as linked with feelings which have a painful component, it should be remembered that from early in the infant's development, the self-representation is closely linked with various forms of object-representation; we cannot consider any shape of the self-representation in isolation. It would probably be more correct to consider (after a certain stage of development has been reached) the actual and ideal shapes of the self-represen-tation in terms of self–object representations; for all psycho-logical object relationships are, in representational terms, self–object relationships.

We went on to point out that a discrepancy between representa-tions of actual and ideal self–object states is linked with feelings of unpleasure or pain. Conversely, states of representational con-gruity (when actual and ideal states more or less coincide) are associated with feelings of well-being and safety.[13] This allowed us to put forward what was perhaps the closest we came to an explicit view of motivation.

> From the point of view of the ego's functioning we are now in a position to say that the prime motivators are conscious or unconscious feeling-states; and that these are, in turn, asso-ciated with various forms of representational congruity or

discrepancy. *The aim of all ego functioning is to reduce conscious or unconscious representational discrepancy and through this to attain or maintain a basic feeling state of well-being* . . . we can say that the ego seeks to maintain a feeling-homeostasis, and this is not to be confused with the notion of energic homeostasis.

In 1974, in an attempt to deal with problems in conceptualizing psychic conflict arising from discrepancies between the structural theory of mental functioning and clinical psychoanalytic experience,[14] I pointed out that the understanding of mental conflict was hindered by "the common error [of equating] the *general* concept of the unconscious wish with the *particular* case of instinctual wishes". But rather than go into the question of the relation between motivation and mental conflict, I shall refer to a paper published in 1978.[15] There emphasis was placed on the role of conscious and unconscious *wishes* as motives in mental functioning: "'instincts' and 'drives' . . . are constructs relating to basic psycho-biological tendencies of the individual, and to the force and energy implicit in these tendencies. From a psychological point of view it is sufficient for us to take, as a basic unit, the *wish*."

In addition to the emphasis on the wish, the link between wishes and object relationships can be reinforced. Object relationships were seen as valued *role relationships,* and those unconscious wishes and wishful phantasies with which we are concerned as psychoanalysts can be regarded as containing mental representations of self and object in interaction.

> Thus, for example, the child who has a wish to cling to the mother, has, as part of this wish, a mental representation of himself clinging to the mother. But he also has, in the content of his wish, a representation of the mother or her substitute responding to his clinging in a particular way, possibly by bending down and embracing him. This formulation is rather different from the idea of a wish consisting of a wishful aim being directed towards the object. The idea of an aim which seeks gratification has to be supplemented by the idea of a *wished-for interaction,* with the wished-for or imagined response of the object being as much a part of the wishful phantasy as the activity of the subject in that wish or phantasy.

Again, we emphasized the role of affects in the self–object interaction.

> There is a substantial part of the mental apparatus which is unconscious in a descriptive sense, but which is not id. Many wishes arise within the mind as responses to motivating forces which are not instinctual. Perhaps the commonest of such motivators are anxiety and other unpleasant affects, but we must equally include the effect of disturbances of inner equilibrium created by stimuli from the outside world (including the subject's own body) as motivators of needs and psychological wishes. The wishes which are aroused may be conscious, but may not be, and very often are not. They may have a drive component, or be developmentally related to the instinctual drives, but this is not a necessary current ingredient of an unconscious wish. Such a wish may, for example, be simply to remove in a particular way whatever is (consciously or unconsciously) identified as a source of discomfort, pain or unpleasure. The wish may be (and often is) motivated by the need to restore feelings of well-being and safety, or may be connected with any one of a whole variety of needs which are very far from those which we normally label as "instinctual". Wishes are aroused by changes in the object world as much as by internal pressures.

It was now possible to speak of the need for "affirmation" by the object world, and in this way to link wishes with object relationships. We said

> If ... a toddler [who has been playing happily with his mother] ... notices that his mother has left the room, a need to perceive her and to interact with her, to hold on to her, will immediately become apparent. This will express itself in the form of a very intense wish with a very definite content. Here we can see that this sort of object relationship is certainly very much a continual wish-fulfilment, in which the wish is to obtain reassurance that the mother is near by (thus fulfilling the need to feel safe). Later in life, the child (and adult) will increasingly be able to make use of an unconscious dialogue with his objects in phantasy in order to gain reassurance.

We took the view that there is a constant need in every individual to externalize his or her "internal objects" (the introjects), to anchor the inner world as far as possible in external reality.*

Externalization of internal objects (with all the distortions that have occurred due to past projections of aspects of the self onto these introjects) can, of course, take place into the world of phantasy, and the resultant phantasies may then be externalized. While all of this is manifestly relevant to the theory of motivation, I need hardly comment that the idea of intense object-related wishes of the sort I have described has not met with universal acceptance.

It is perhaps useful at this point to turn to some classical formulations in this area to see where we stand in relation to them. What can be more appropriate than to turn to Anna Freud? Some years ago a group of us at the Hampstead Clinic met regularly with Anna Freud to discuss her 1936 book on *The Ego and the Mechanisms of Defence,*[16] and for many of us the reconsideration of what we had read many times in the past was extremely enlightening. We were able to see things in the text that we had been blind to before, but were now glaringly obvious to us.[17] In a chapter in Anna Freud's *Defences* book on "Orientation of the Processes of Defence According to the Source of Anxiety and Danger", under the heading of "Motives for the Defence Against Instincts", she describes how the ego's mechanisms of defence are motivated by anxieties of various sorts. The adult neurotic's defences are prompted, she says, by superego anxiety. The superego, Anna Freud writes,

> is the mischief-maker which prevents the ego's coming to a friendly understanding with the instincts. It sets up an ideal standard, according to which sexuality is prohibited and aggression pronounced to be antisocial. It demands a degree

---

* Much later it became clear that there is a need to distinguish between the internal objects and the unconscious phantasies formed *in the present*—that is, current phantasies derived from the internal self-object relationships. It is the relationships between self and object embodied in such current phantasies that are externalized (as, for example, in the transference). From a theoretical point of view the distinction is important, although at times it is convenient to speak of the externalization of the introjects. At other times this may be misleading. This issue is discussed in later chapters.

of sexual renunciation and restriction of aggression which is incompatible with psychic health. The ego is completely deprived of its independence and reduced to the status of an instrument for the execution of the superego's wishes; the result is that it becomes hostile to instinct and *incapable of enjoyment*.

Anna Freud then goes on to write of objective anxiety—anxiety felt by the child as arising from the outside world—as a motive for defence. The ego's defences can be "motivated by dread of the outside world". She then describes the ego's dread of the strength of the instincts as a source of anxiety, and therefore a motivator of defence, but points out that the *source* of the anxiety is not what is important; what is important is the anxiety itself, which then prompts defence.

In that chapter Anna Freud introduces the idea of defence against affect (as opposed to defence against instinct). She says,

> There is, however, another and more primitive relation between the ego and the affects which has no counterpart in that of the ego to the instincts. . . . If the ego has nothing to object to in a particular instinctual process and so does not ward off an affect on that ground, its attitude toward it will be determined entirely by the pleasure principle: *it will welcome pleasurable affects and defend itself against painful ones*. . . . It is all the more ready to ward off affects associated with prohibited sexual impulses if these affects happen to be distressing, e.g., pain, longing, mourning. On the other hand it may resist a prohibition somewhat longer in the case of positive affects, simply because they are pleasurable, or may sometimes be persuaded to tolerate them for a short time when they make a sudden irruption into consciousness. [italics added]

Anna Freud now refers to *The Ego and the Id*[18] and to *Inhibitions, Symptoms and Anxiety* and quotes Freud in his statement that

> What it is that the ego fears from the external world and from the libidinal danger cannot be specified; we know that the fear is of being overwhelmed or annihilated, but it cannot be grasped analytically.

What is true for the motives for defence must also be true for the motives for adaptation in general. In a sense everything we do has a defensive aspect, and all defensive activity can certainly be regarded as (intrapsychically) adaptive.

On looking back, it becomes clear that Freud's second theory of anxiety, introduced in 1926, in which anxiety was seen as a danger signal to the ego, functioning to warn it of the eventual possibility of being traumatically overwhelmed, was a major stimulus to Anna Freud's formulations. We find ourselves very much at one with Ernst Kris, who said in 1947 that he was convinced that the reformulation by Freud in 1926 of a considerable set of his previous hypotheses reaches further than was realized at the time of publication, possibly by Freud himself.[19]

I can now return to the point at which this circuitous journey started and recall Anna Freud's criticism of the idea that the patient I described might have become deaf because of the need to recreate the presence of a highly critical internal grandparent figure in her current external world. Her criticism was based, as she put it, on the "world of difference between the mild, all-pervading 'functional' pleasure of perception and a drive, an instinctual urge, such as the one for passive, masochistic experience". She went on to say: "The latter is an id-urge and, as such, can set action in motion; the former is nothing of the kind, that is, does not belong to the instinct world." It is interesting that Anna Freud could permit herself to say this, because it testifies to a split that has existed in psychoanalytic thought in the area of the theory of motivation ever since the publication of Freud's *Inhibitions, Symptoms and Anxiety* in 1926. On the one hand, it is as if we have to maintain the idea that all driving forces in behaviour are motivated by the instinctual drives or by derivatives of the drives, and of course the first theory of anxiety, in which anxiety was seen as transformed libido, fitted the theory well. On the other hand, the revision of the theory of anxiety in 1926 put into our theory a formulation that fitted much better with clinical experience—namely, that anxiety could function as a signal of danger that could initiate intense defensive and adaptive activity. Anna Freud has made it abundantly clear that unpleasant affect *of any sort* can set action in motion, and by no stretch of the imagination can we simply equate unpleasant affect with instinctual drive urges; nor is instinctual drive tension the only source of uncomfortable or painful affect. So Anna Freud has presented us with another set of motives, the motives for defence and adaptation, many of which she spelled out in *The Ego and the Mechanisms of Defence*.

In the development of our thought in this area the different theories of motivation have been kept quite separate, and psychoanalysts have moved easily from one to another, following the dictates of their particular theoretical and clinical needs at the time. So we have a theory of motivation that equates motives with instinctual drives—a theory that goes back to the end of the last century. Simultaneously, we have a theory of motivation based upon unpleasant affect—in particular, anxiety—as a driving force in human behaviour, deriving from the radical reformulations in Freud's *Inhibitions, Symptoms and Anxiety*. These two theories need, in my view, to be brought face to face and the differences between them dealt with. I believe that a psychoanalytic psychology of motivation that does not take instinctual drives into account is an impoverished psychology—but so is a drive psychology that does not recognize motives other than the drives.

It could, of course, be argued that Freud's pleasure–unpleasure principle does act as a unifying principle in this area. Yet, as Max Schur has effectively shown,[20] the pleasure–unpleasure principle has been used differently at different times, essentially either in an economic–energic context or linked with the death instinct and the Nirvana Principle.* Schur, who proposed that the pleasure and unpleasure principles be divorced rather than brought together in marriage, also commented as follows:

> Few analysts, . . . who use the concepts pleasure–unpleasure, pleasure–pain principle, spell out precisely which of Freud's formulations they are actually referring to. This is especially confusing in any consideration of the relationship between the regulating principles and the affects pleasure and unpleasure, and in any discussion of those modes of functioning which Freud tried to explain in *Beyond the Pleasure Principle*.[21]

---

*Freud's Nirvana Principle, introduced in 1920 in *Beyond the Pleasure Principle* (Standard Edition, 20), referred to his assumption that accumulated energies had a tendency towards complete discharge—a state of zero excitation. He then saw this state as being reached through the operation of the "death instinct."

The papers referred to earlier suggest that the urge to gain feelings of well-being and safety are very powerful, although such feelings lack the conscious or unconscious excitement associated with instinctual drive gratification. The need to gain feelings of safety and well-being must at times be stronger than the urge to experience the feelings associated with instinctual satisfaction, because otherwise we would simply be gratifying our instinctual drive wishes as they arise. The whole of the reality principle is, after all, based upon the need to delay instinctual gratification because it is unsafe. What is it, then, that can make feelings of non-sensual well-being or security more attractive than, let us say, the direct sexual pleasure associated with sexual drive satisfaction?

Perhaps we can move further forward by making use of the idea of "value cathexis" referred to earlier. This is ultimately the feeling state with which a particular mental representation is invested, which is a measure of its positive or negative attractiveness, of (in a sense) the pressure that motivates one towards it. An object or an activity can have a sexual erotic value cathexis, but it can also have a cathexis of love, which is not quite the same thing. Equally, it can have a cathexis of anger and a cathexis of hate, and here again the two are not identical. Perhaps most significantly in the present context, *it can have a cathexis of safety or a cathexis of well-being*.

It must be apparent by now that the idea of an affective value cathexis is relevant to our discussion of motivation and consistent with the line of thought described earlier. I should like to approach the end of this chapter by trying to tie a further pair of loose ends together, and I want to do this by adding the proposition that the value cathexis—and therefore the attractiveness—of an activity or of an object is a variable quantity; it can even vary from one moment to the next. The value cathexis attached to a particular wished-for state, goal, aim, or object is a function, not only of the intrinsic potential for pleasant feelings associated with that state, goal, aim, or object, but also of an added investment provided by the need to do away with *unpleasant* feelings. These unpleasant affects arise from instinctual tensions and from threats and dangers of the most varied sort. Foremost among these painful affects is anxiety, no matter whether its source is instinctual or otherwise.

Let me formulate this in another way. Imagine the normal child who feels safe when with his or her mother. We can say that the mother is invested with a certain affective value cathexis of safety for the child. Margaret Mahler[22] has described very vividly how the toddler "checks back to mother" so as to receive "refuelling", and we can say that in this way the child modulates his level of safety feeling and maintains it at an appropriate level. When the toddler falls and hurts himself, or when he suddenly loses sight of mother, or is threatened in some other way, her value as a source of safety feeling rises dramatically, for the feeling of safety with which the mother is invested also contains the element of *the absence of non-safety, the absence of danger*. The same sort of fluctuation in cathexis of value occurs, of course, in relation to the drives. The stronger the sexual urge, the greater the value attached to the sexual object or activity, to a particular self–object interaction. Here again, the sexual cathexis of value attached to the object at that particular time contains the affective promise of relief from sexual tension. It is extremely common in our psychoanalytic clinical work to see impulses of all sorts compounded of the two kinds of elements I have been describing.

The view of motivation put forward here provides, I believe, a framework for the closer integration of object relations theories with the drive aspects of motivation and provides us with an understanding of object relationships that is more satisfactory than the simple formulation that objects are cathected with libido. In every situation of anxiety, for instance, there is a reaching towards the object that can provide safety, and this applies as much to the phantasy objects derived from the introjects as to external objects. This was very much the case with the patient I described earlier in this chapter. By being deaf, she created the illusion of the presence of the object, and we can say that the impulse to interact with the object in her own particular way was intense. True, she paid a price in pain and suffering in this relationship, but the function of the object as a source of safety and reassurance against threat of abandonment and disintegration outweighed all other factors. Of course, while we can also assume that she might have had a perverse sexual investment in the suffering she endured, this element was not, to my mind, the major motivating factor. This is absolutely in line with the clinical reality that, in our masochistic patients, the analysis of guilt-motivated self-damaging behaviour often plays a far greater role than the analysis of perverse sexual pleasure—and that guilt, as an affect, is a form of anxiety. So my answer to Anna Freud's letter would be, "Yes, you are right, when there is no threat then feelings of safety are mild when compared with instinctual pleasure. But situations of safety, particularly those associated with familiar interaction with the (internal or external) object, can become even more attractive than instinctual drive satisfaction when danger threatens. No one has demonstrated this more convincingly than you have done in *The Ego and the Mechanisms of Defence*."

I want to emphasize the belief that we need to develop an approach to motivation that allows us to take into account much more satisfactorily than in the past what we know about external and internal object relationships. We know now that it is impossible to contain a theory of object relations in a theoretical framework in which all motivation is reduced to drives, and the answer must surely lie not in a distortion of what we know about object relationships, but in a modification of our essential theoretical framework to take other sources of motivation into account.

CHAPTER TWO

The striving for "identity of perception"

Introduction

The idea of wish-fulfilment through the attainment of an identity of perception is a key concept in the link between unconscious wishes on the one hand and object relationships on the other. It provides a basis for the notions that follow, of actualization and role-responsiveness, and their relation to countertransference.

In an earlier version, this chapter was given as a Freud Lecture in Vienna in 1975 on the 75th anniversary of *The Interpretation of Dreams*.[1] When one reads Freud's book today, one can only marvel at the boldness and incisiveness of his thinking. It stands as a monument to him, though it was one of his earliest works. It has provided material for psychoanalytic scholars to work on and to study, a process that will continue for many generations. At the time of its publication, the book put forward the most radical of theoretical formulations, simultaneously raising a multitude of questions, some of which were answered by Freud himself, others by later workers, while many remain unanswered.

A point made by Freud in the famous seventh chapter of *The Interpretation of Dreams* but never fully developed by him in his later writings provides the theme of this chapter and is a foundation for many of the arguments put forward in this book. It is the idea of the "identity of perception" [*Wahrnehmungsidentität*], and it is possible to show that this idea, first presented in a discussion of dreams, may be generalized to a whole realm of experience and behaviour.

A short historical review precedes brief comments on the psychoanalytic concepts of unconscious phantasy and unconscious wish. This is followed by a consideration of some of Freud's thoughts about the identity of perception, with special reference to the idea of wish-fulfilment. The remarks made by Freud, on wish-fulfilment gained through the attainment of an identity of perception, provide a basis for looking at psychoanalytic theory from a different perspective—one that is extremely relevant to the concept of internal object.

* * *

Even before the publication of *The Interpretation of Dreams*, Freud had elaborated the idea of a dissociation of the mind as a consequence of processes of *defence*.[2] In one form or another, the idea of the need to protect the ego—that is, to protect consciousness from being overwhelmed by something unpleasant and overpowering—has remained central to psychoanalytic theory. Because of the increasing "structuralization" of the term *ego* in Freud's later work and the use of the term as a specifically structural concept in much psychoanalytic psychology, it is often forgotten that Freud's early use of the term was closely linked with consciousness. This link remained implicit in much of Freud's work even after the introduction of the structural theory.[3] There is a good case for returning more explicitly to the idea that the protection of consciousness is one of the most important functions of the mental apparatus. So, for example, the idea of a "traumatic experience" as the overpowering of consciousness by painful and uncontrollable sensations from any source would appear to have more clinical value than the definition of trauma as the helpless (structural) ego being overwhelmed by uncontrollable excitation.[4]

From Freud's correspondence with Wilhelm Fliess we now know more of the circumstances of his move away from the "trauma" theory of neurosis towards a theory based on the idea of internal conflict over the gratification of sexual (libidinal) drive impulses. His letters[5] show the way in which he was inescapably drawn in 1897 to his new ideas because of his work with his patients, in particular his "chief patient", himself. Freud's findings from his self-analysis, using a procedure that consisted predominantly of the painstaking analysis of his own dreams and of his associations to the various elements in them, were probably the most important factors in his turning away from the trauma theory. However, even before the giving up of the trauma theory of pathogenesis, Freud had seen daydreams (conscious daydream phantasies) as wish-fulfilments—as shown, for example, in his description of the case of Anna O.[6] "She embellished her life . . . by indulging in systematic day-dreaming, which she described as her 'private theatre'."

The publication of *The Interpretation of Dreams* in 1900 provided the basis for a "topographical" model of mental functioning, involving the "systems" Unconscious (*Ucs.*), Preconscious (*Pcs.*), and Perceptual–Conscious (*Pcpt.–Cs.* or *Cs.*). The system Unconscious was also known as the "dynamic" Unconscious. This model seemed to account not only for the psychological processes in dreaming, but also for the production of a whole variety of other surface derivatives of unconscious processes.[7] From today's perspective one might comment that *The Interpretation of Dreams* could equally well have been written as *The Interpretation of Phantasies*, *The Interpretation of Symptoms*, and so on, but in that phase of his work dreams provided Freud with the most readily accessible path to the depths of the unconscious mind. The interpretation of dreams was the "royal road to the Unconscious", but Freud recognized that the processes involved in the construction of daydreams, neurotic symptoms, artistic and literary creations, sublimations, and the like were in essence the same as those that entered into the formation of the dream.

The introduction of the topographical model in 1900 resulted in a fundamental shift of interest to the clinical and theoretical importance of sexual wishes and wish-fulfilling daydreams, which might or might not be within the patient's conscious awareness. It could be said that throughout this long phase the fundamental function of the mental apparatus was seen as that of harnessing the instinctual drives, *thus protecting consciousness*. Freud was able to show relatively early[8] that, as the child develops, this "harnessing" of the drives increasingly takes knowledge of reality into account (though such knowledge may be extremely distorted). Nevertheless, drive-invested wishes could be gratified in disguised form. The nature of this disguised gratification and of wish-fulfilment is commented upon later in this chapter.

The enormity of the change introduced with the topographical model and the publication of *The Interpretation of Dreams* cannot be emphasized strongly enough. The individual was seen, to a great extent, to be at the mercy of sexual drive impulses arising *from within himself*. These impulses could not be allowed direct expression after early childhood but could show themselves only indirectly as disguised surface manifestations of instinctual wishes arising from the depths of the mental apparatus. They could instigate conflict, and the attempted solutions to such conflicts could result either in normal derivatives (such as conscious daydreams) or in pathology. Conflicts could come about because of the enduring influence of the *past* within the mind of the individual and because of his need to take his knowledge of present-day and anticipated future reality into account in the interest of self-preservation (that is, to protect consciousness). Processes such as defence against the direct expression of crude libidinal wishes, their "censorship", transformation, and disguised gratification were highlighted. Throughout the phase in which the topographical model was the basic theoretical frame of reference, such phenomena as dreams, daydreams, symptoms, character traits, works of art, and other forms of expression were regarded as *compromise-formations* between instinctual wishes and all the forces that oppose instinctual gratification (or the awareness of gratification); they were regarded as distorted and disguised *derivatives* of unconscious instinctual wishes.

The creation of conscious daydreams is a major form of wish-fulfilment available to us during waking life when, for one reason or another, gratification, satisfaction, or fulfilment is unobtainable from the external world. Because the direct gratification of a wish may prove threatening, the defensive and compensatory turning to daydreams as a form of wish-fulfilment in the face of internally imposed restrictions may occur. Nowadays, as is stressed throughout this book, we can say that it is not only instinctual wishes seeking gratification that can be involved in conflict, but the whole range of (descriptively) unconscious wishes, including those related to the avoidance of unpleasant affects of all sorts and to the preservation of the individual's narcissism, feelings of self-esteem, safety and security, feelings of mastery, and so on. This also means that we include in our idea of unconscious wishes the vast range of wishes prompted or motivated by conscious or unconscious changes in the individual's affective states.[9] As Kernberg put it: "Affects, operating as the earliest motivational system, are therefore intimately linked with the fixation by memory of an internalized world of object relations".[10]

Much daydreaming goes on at a very low level of conscious awareness, eluding our grasp as we attempt to focus our attention on the daydream phantasies. We are probably all aware of this phenomenon, and it seems likely that many (if not most) of us spend much of our time in wish-fulfilling daydream thinking. Freud saw the daydream as "a wish-fulfilling product of the imagination, which is known not to be real"[11]—perhaps, one might say, "a wish-fulfilling thought known not to be true", for phantasy is, as Freud pointed out in "Formulations on the Two Principles of Mental Functioning", a form of thought. The conscious daydream does not have the same intensity or vividness as normal or hallucinatory perception and is consequently intrinsically less satisfying than the gratifying experiences provided by material reality or by hallucination. Like the dream, the daydream is not normally *simply* a repetition of past satisfying experiences, although at times it may be. Memories of past experiences may be based predominantly on the way the individual's wishes were gratified in interaction with material reality—particularly with the important persons in the child's environment; but daydreams may also be linked with *memories of daydreams that have been satisfying or comforting in the past.* Usually, however, it is a new and disguised construction, though it is often (to borrow a term Freud used about transference) a "new edition" of an older work.[12]

So much for conscious daydreams. But what of unconscious phantasies? First, we have those phantasies that were once daydream wish-fulfilments but have subsequently been repressed; consequently, they tend to function and be treated in the same way as repressed *memories* of satisfied wishes. Such daydream phantasies, which are perfectly acceptable to the child at one time, may later be repressed because they arouse conflict and are regarded as unacceptable to consciousness.[13] A typical example would be an oedipal girl's conscious daydream of living alone with her father and devotedly looking after him, her mother having disappeared from the scene through death or illness. Such a common conscious daydream will often be repressed later, changing its status to being (or entering into the content of) an unconscious wish.

This brings us to those phantasies that are new or developmentally late unconscious creations, involving unconscious secondary process thinking.[14] In the formation of these phantasies, current preoccupations (which may or may not be reality-based) are involved, conflict enters, childhood impulses and solutions are revived, the defences play a prominent role, current or recent experiences may be used, and secondary thought processes, varying from the most primitive to the relatively sophisticated, are employed. It is worth noting that the development of certain highly organized defences—in particular, unconscious rationalization—also testifies to the existence of unconscious secondary process activity.

From the point of view of Freud's structural model, it is easy to attribute the formation of these unconscious phantasies to the unconscious ego. It is more difficult to place them within the framework of the topographical theory in its 1900 version without considering Freud's postulation of a "second censorship" between the Conscious and Preconscious systems.[15] The "second censorship"—or the defensive and censoring work of the "structural" ego—can be regarded as aimed at protecting consciousness. This is an important notion for psychoanalytic theory because it allows us to conceive of sophisticated unconscious processes (strictly speaking, processes in the "non-existential realm"[16]) producing and constructing experiential content that is "scanned", assessed in terms of its acceptability to consciousness, continuously modified and disguised, and given a degree of "plausibility" and rational organization in order to make it "consciousness-syntonic". This point is worth stressing because of the extremely widespread tendency in psychoanalytic thinking to equate, quite incorrectly, all content that is, *descriptively* speaking, unconscious with the *system* Unconscious of the topographical model. (Some confusion exists between the "dynamic" unconscious and the "descriptive" unconscious.[17] In Freud's topographical model the part of the mind which is "descriptively" unconscious includes the "system" Preconscious.)

In discussing his concept of a "second censorship" in *The Interpretation of Dreams*, Freud speaks of

> a second and more discriminating regulation, which is even able to oppose the former one [the censorship between the dynamic Unconscious and the Preconscious, responsible for the infantile amnesia], and which perfects the efficiency of the apparatus by enabling it, in contradiction to its original plan, to cathect and work over even what is associated with the release of unpleasure. We learn from the psychology of the neuroses that these processes of regulation . . . play a great part in the functional activity of the apparatus.

Curiously, many analysts exhibit great resistance to the idea of unconscious—that is, preconscious, and consequently *descriptively unconscious*—secondary process functioning (a concept that can be regarded as comprising all levels of organized cognitive processes), although the assumption that it does occur is evident in their clinical work. We may label such processes as "preconscious" or speak of the "workings of the unconscious ego" to describe these phenomena, but whatever term or model of the mind we use, the "second censorship", just below the level of consciousness, has to be considered. The point may perhaps be best illustrated by a piece of clinical material.

> A patient reported that he had seen a parcel left on the doorstep of the analyst's house and commented that the delivery-man must have been impatient because he did not wait for the parcel to be received. Later in the session he remarked on recent bomb explosions in London and on letter bombs that had been sent to prominent Jews. On the basis of this and other material it was possible for the analyst to point out that perhaps, on seeing the parcel, the patient had the thought that it contained a bomb and

that the analyst would be blown up, so that the patient could start his holiday earlier than planned. Here one can postulate the existence of unconscious wishful thinking involving a notion of cause and effect. Incidentally, this patient later remembered wishing that the analyst would cancel the remainder of the sessions and feeling impatient about having to wait for his vacation. Subsequently the patient's childhood anger with his father for making him study during the holidays emerged in the analysis. This was later traced to his oedipal hostility towards his father and his fear of father's revenge, and eventually to an earlier traumatic experience.

In referring here to unconscious phantasy thoughts it should be made clear that although these may be updated versions of past wish-fulfilling daydreams that had once been conscious and were subsequently repressed, they are usually heavily influenced by a number of factors. These include current unconscious conflicts and concerns, the use of secondary process thinking, the unconscious childhood assumptions and theories of the individual, the patient's organized internal relationships to his introjects, the persistence of his childhood wishes, his tendency to make use of past solutions to problems and conflicts, as well as many other factors.

For present purposes we need only be concerned with the unconscious phantasy as a particular type of organized unconscious *derivative* of more primitive (particularly childhood) wishes and impulses and the unconscious object relationships (and associated feelings) involved in such strivings. Essentially the unconscious phantasy can be regarded as an organized, disguised, unconscious modification and elaboration of an unsatisfied wish, which may or may not be "instinctual". Elements in the person's past and present subjective experience will, of course, be embroidered into the unconscious wishful phantasy, but the distinction between such phantasies and other unconscious thoughts that bear less of a special relation to wish-fulfilment[18] has not been considered. From the point in its development when an unconscious wishful phantasy has evolved, it is constantly being modified, although it will tend to retain its past central core. Just as the wish has a force behind it propelling it towards "fulfilment", so is there a force behind its unconscious derivative—that is, behind the organized unconscious phantasy. It is worth reminding ourselves that the pressure behind what Freud in *The Interpretation of Dreams* called the "wishful phantasy" need not be that of an instinctual drive—it can equally be the need to avoid painful experiences (such as anxiety and guilt) and to preserve safety and well-being.[19]

The unconscious phantasy (in the sense in which the term is used here) can be regarded as representing a wish-fulfilment, but, paradoxically, at the same time it represents an unfulfilled wish. It is a wish-fulfilment in that it is an unconsciously constructed "solution" to conflicts aroused by the more primitive wish it represents. On the other hand, the unconscious phantasy persists precisely because it is also an unfulfilled wish, and the experience of it as fulfilled can only be temporary. (In contrast to the unconscious phantasy, the conscious daydream phantasy functions much more as a wish-fulfilment.) It is likely that most active unconscious phantasies eventually find a form of surface expression that may have to be so heavily disguised—or expressed so subtly in action—that the "second censorship" is deceived. This shows itself in the derivatives we observe in the "classical" psychoanalytic situation in, for example, free associations, acting out, dreams, and transference phenomena. The persistence of dominant or "core" unconscious phantasies is probably due to many factors, including the ways in which significant elements in the particular unconscious phantasy wish have been gratified in the past and the enduring internal structural organization of the person's unconscious memories, assumptions, theories, object relationships, and preferred defence mechanisms. (This aspect of the mind's organization has been considered to be located in the "non-experiential realm"[20]—see Chapter 4.)

It may be useful to comment further on the apparent contradiction inherent in the notion of "wishful phantasy", in that the concept embraces the notions both of an unsatisfied wish and simultaneously of a wish-fulfilment. The answer to the puzzle may lie in the fact that the ego's capacity for distinguishing between reality and phantasy is not in constant use during waking life. It may seem as if it is, but this is because the function of being able to distinguish between what is reality and what is not can be called into action extremely rapidly (unless one's mind is clouded by sleep or fatigue or is affected by drugs, or there is an ego defect of the sort found in psychosis). During the process of phantasying (whether conscious daydreaming or unconscious phantasying), this aspect of reality-testing is partially suspended, although we can normally tune into reality very quickly indeed. So, for short periods of time, while reality awareness is partially suspended, the wish is experienced as though it has been fulfilled. This resembles the night-time dream experience, although the daydream does not normally come anywhere near having the perceptual intensity of the nocturnal hallucination that constitutes the dream. When the daydreaming state is interrupted for any reason, we have an unfulfilled wish rather than a wish-fulfilment.

To recapitulate: the unconscious wishful phantasies referred to here are created with the specific aim of circumventing the "censorship" protecting consciousness, but to do this they may have to undergo a whole series of modifications before being expressed in one or other type of surface derivative. They are not built on primary process functioning alone but use the capacity for a whole variety of organized unconscious forms of thinking. They are, of course, significantly modified by the defences mobilized to control the feeling states within the experiential realm of the individual (see Chapter 4). They may or may not make use of the individual's knowledge of external reality, and if they are at any significant distance from consciousness (in the "topographical" sense), they will not possess the "hallmark of unreality" that is characteristic of conscious daydreams.[21] The conception of the unconscious phantasy given here is very different from the Kleinian view expressed in 1948 by Susan Isaacs,[22] who regarded *any* unconscious mental content as "unconscious phantasy".

The nocturnal dream differs from the daydream in that it is a hallucinatory experience, *is believed to be real at the time*, and involves more primitive mechanisms than the relatively logical and coherent wish-fulfilling daydream. Moreover, while daydreams may fulfil quite conscious wishes as well as unconscious ones, the underlying wish or wishful phantasy fulfilled in the nocturnal dream is, in the older child and adult, disguised in its manifest dream content, as it is not acceptable to consciousness in its "latent" form. The "second censorship" operates even during sleep, attempting to fulfil its task of protecting consciousness.

Reference was made earlier to the surface manifestations of the derivatives of unconscious wishes and wishful phantasies as "forms of expression". This term has been chosen advisedly, for the main emphasis in psychoanalysis, particularly in the years before the structural model was introduced but also since, has been on the understanding of the meaning of surface behaviour and conscious experience in terms of the vicissitudes of unconscious instinctual drives and wishes being forced forward to surface expression. External reality was always considered,[23] but because of the nature of psychoanalytic technique the microscope of psychoanalytic investigation has for the most part been directed from outside inwards, towards tracing the way in which the individual's repressed infantile instinctual wishes find their expression on the surface. From this standpoint, the view of the role of the dream as a form of surface expression, as a derivative of impulses and wishes moving from the depths to the surface, has been felt to be particularly important. This view of derivatives of unconscious forces and content can be regarded as a *centrifugal* one, a reflection of forces moving outwards towards the periphery of the mental apparatus, consistent with Freud's theory of energy "discharge". Later it will be clear why the centrifugal view of the dream process is insufficient.

Wish-fulfilment and "identity of perception"

In the famous seventh chapter of *The Interpretation of Dreams,* Freud pointed out that instinctual wishes could be fulfilled by means of achieving an *identity of perception*. The simplest statement of this process is that the primitive wish has as its aim the re-experiencing, through perception, of a past situation that brought about instinctual gratification. Thus, for example, if memory traces of the experience of being satisfactorily fed are laid down in the young infant, the oral instinctual wish when the baby is hungry again would be a striving to re-experience, through the perceptual apparatus, a situation that is perceptually identical with the earlier subjective experience of gratification—that is, with the satisfying experience of being fed. In *The Interpretation of Dreams*, Freud says of the hungry baby:

> ... the excitation arising from an internal need is not due to a force producing a *momentary* impact but to one which is in continuous operation. A change can only come about if in some way or other (in the case of the baby, through outside help) an "experience of satisfaction" can be achieved which puts an end to the internal stimulus. An essential component of this experience of satisfaction is a particular perception (that of nourishment, in our example) the mnemic image of which remains associated thenceforward with the memory trace of the excitation produced by the need. As a result of the link that has thus been established, next time this need arises a psychical impulse will at once emerge which will seek to re-cathect[*] the mnemic image of the perception and to re-evoke the perception itself, that is to say, to re-establish the situation of the original satisfaction. An impulse of this kind is what we call a wish; the reappearance of the perception is the fulfilment of the wish. . . . Nothing prevents us from assuming that there was a primitive state . . . in which wishing ended in hallucinating. Thus the aim of this first psychical activity was to produce a "perceptual identity"—a repetition of the perception which was linked with the satisfaction of the need.

In this context, "experience" means *subjective* experience (the German *Erlebnis*, not *Erfahrung*, although both are translated by the English word "experience"). It is obvious, as Freud points out, that in the case of a biological need the hallucinated experience of satisfaction can last only for a moment, because the incessant pressure of the biological need will, after a little while, cause the person to feel acute unpleasure. Freud returned to the topic in "Formulations on the Two Principles of Mental Functioning", remarking that, "the state of psychical rest was originally disturbed by the peremptory demands of internal needs. When this happened, whatever was thought of (wished for) was simply presented in a hallucinatory

---

* Freud's idea was that the re-cathexis (re-investment) of the memory trace with libidinal energy activated it into becoming the content of a libidinal wish.

manner, just as still happens today with our dream-thoughts every night."

From the simple proposition that the wish seeks fulfilment through the achievement of an experience that is perceptually identical with the earlier "experience of satisfaction", Freud went on to show in *The Interpretation of Dreams* how the process of wish-fulfilment through a simple hallucination has to be modified. He discusses the "roundabout path to wish-fulfilment that has been made necessary by experience" and describes the development of *thought* as a substitute for the hallucinatory wish. As he saw it, it is above all the *dream* that shows us something of the more direct path to wish-fulfilment through hallucination.

With mental development after early childhood, even the gaining of perceptual identity in the dream does not represent the simple hallucinatory repetition of a previous perception of gratification. The censorship has developed to protect consciousness and to guard sleep, and so what we find is a perceptual identity *thoroughly disguised* by the operation of a whole variety of both primitive and more sophisticated mechanisms. Simple infantile experiences of gratification have been supplemented by highly complicated wishes such as those characteristic of the Oedipus complex and its derivatives. Daydreams once tolerated by the young child have become dangerous and have undergone repression, adding to the wishful content of unconscious strivings.

We can elaborate on Freud's idea of the wish striving for perceptual identity—as occurs classically in the dream—by saying that the wish-fulfilment implicit in *any* surface expression of unconscious wishes or wishful phantasies is not only an outward expression, not only a breakthrough or irruption of the fulfilled unconscious wish in a disguised form, not only a centrifugal process. There is a *centripetal* element that is of equal importance. In order for the derivative to function as a wish-fulfilment, it has also to involve the conscious or unconscious *perception* of what has reached the surface. (It is possible to speculate that the rapid eye movements that occur during the dream phase of sleep—that is, REM sleep—may be biological "givens" connected with the *perception* of the dream rather than with its creation.)

What is meant is simply this: a dream would be useless to the dreamer unless, at the time, he could also function as the observer of the dream. Similarly, a daydream would be valueless as a wish-fulfilment unless it were in some way perceived (perception should here be distinguished from attention). A work of art would have no function in satisfying an unconscious wish unless the artist were aware of the act of creating and of the qualities of the creation itself. If we follow this argument to its logical conclusion, even those symptoms regarded by Freud as derivatives of the dynamic Unconscious in the form of compromise formations would have no value as wish-fulfilments unless the patients, at some level, perceived them.

If wish-fulfilment comes about through the attainment, in a highly disguised and symbolic form, of an identity of perception, we are faced with the problem of how it is that this is brought about. How is it that to dream that some strange person presents another with a posy of flowers, while the dreamer stands aside as an observer, can provide the gratification of a sexual wish during the dream? How is it that the construction of a work of art, full of symbolic and disguised wish-fulfilments, can effect the gratification of crude unconscious wishes by means of the expression *and the perception* of the symbolic representations?

Probably the answer may lie in an ability of the individual to understand the symbolic meaning of his own dream (or of any other "derivative", for that matter) *unconsciously*. What is crucial here is the absolute necessity for the person to protect his own consciousness from his unconscious knowledge. The point that needs to be stressed is that perception can provide gratification and that it can do so, not only by representing the wished-for situation, but also by doing so in a *disguised* form. While perception can provide gratification only momentarily in the case of pressing biological needs, for psychological needs and wishes (including wishful phantasies) direct or indirect gratification by way of perception can be much more substantially obtained; moreover, it can be reached *symbolically*. We have only to consider the phenomenon of sublimation[24] and the way in which gratifications can be gained indirectly by "proxy"[25] to be aware of this process of unconscious wish-fulfilment occurring without direct bodily stimulation. Some of these points are considered again in Chapter 3.

A comment made by Freud in "Formulations on the Two Principles of Mental Functioning" is of some interest. He says:

An artist is originally a man who turns away from reality because he cannot come to terms with the renunciation of instinctual satisfaction which it at first demands, and who allows his erotic and ambitious wishes full play in the life of phantasy. He finds the way back to reality, however, from this world of phantasy by making use of special gifts to mould his phantasies into truths of a new kind, which are valued by men as precious reflections of reality. Thus in a certain fashion he actually becomes the hero, the king, the creator, or the favourite he desired to be, without following the long roundabout path of making real alterations in the external world. But he can only achieve this because other men feel the same dissatisfaction as he does with the renunciation demanded by reality, and because that dissatisfaction, which results from the replacement of the pleasure principle by the reality principle, is itself a part of reality.

What is the nature of the "reality" and the "truth" that can provide the fulfilment of unconscious wishes and wishful phantasies? It can only be something "known" as reality or truth, something perceived, or a conclusion drawn in the mind of the individual concerned, based on information reaching him by way of his sense organs and his perceptual apparatus. The "truths of a new kind" referred to by Freud must surely be psychological data of a sort that may be very far from the sort of data provided by direct bodily stimulation, for example by stimulation of the erotogenic zones.

In Chapter 3 an effort is made to reinforce the link between transference and countertransference from the starting-point of a definition of transference that includes the patient's attempts to manipulate the analyst into actions and reactions that represented for the patient a concealed repetition of earlier experiences and relationships. Countertransference is seen as a compromise between the analyst's own tendencies and his response to the role that the patient attempts to force upon him. Transference and countertransference, as discussed in Chapter 3, are specific instances of the more general phenomenon of *actualization*. The term is used in the dictionary sense of the word, not in the specific technical senses in which it has been used by certain writers. The *Oxford English Dictionary* defines *actualization* as "a making actual; a realization in action or fact" and to *actualize* as "to make actual, to convert into an actual fact, to realize in action". This concept is discussed more fully in Chapter 3, but it is appropriate to comment now that *we can regard all wish-fulfilment as brought about through some form of actualization.* The commonest way of making something "real" or "actual" is to act on the real world so that our perception comes to correspond to the wished-for reality; we may also act upon ourselves so as to attain this correspondence. Commonly we do both, but there are other forms of actualization. We may include *illusional* actualization, in which the perceptual process distorts the sensory data arising from the external world in the direction of wish-fulfilment, although normally such an illusion can be corrected by later experience. If it cannot, we have *delusional* actualization, a process that is by no means restricted to psychotics. Wish-fulfilment through *hallucinatory* actualization is, of course, common in psychosis. A major form is *symbolic* actualization, in which the symbol—for example, the wearing of a uniform—represents the fulfilment of a wish. Actualization through *daydreams* is normally less satisfying than gratification by way of direct perceptual experience, although much will depend on the degree of anxiety aroused by the real experience (some people, particularly adolescents, prefer actualization through daydreaming to experiencing it in reality), on the sensory intensity of the daydream images and the capacity of the individual to suspend "disbelief" temporarily during daydreaming.

There are many implications of the point of view put forward in this chapter that cannot be systematically considered here. However, what is discussed is an approach to the consideration of interpersonal relationships, without discarding the framework of intrapsychic psychoanalytic psychology, by considering the processes involved in each person's attempts to actualize his conscious and unconscious wishes. *These are, in turn, intimately connected with the object relationships involved in the individual's wishes and phantasies.*

The roles of perception and actualization in wish-fulfilment also enable us to understand more of the nature and function of neurotic symptoms. To the extent that the symptom can be regarded as a derivative of a wishful phantasy not acceptable to the individual's consciousness, we would have to say that the symptom is not only a disguised "surface expression" of the unconscious phantasy, but also a source of perceptual information providing a concealed and symbolic identity of perception in relation to the unconscious wish it satisfies. If, in addition, we consider that an unconscious interaction with another person is an integral part of the wishful phantasy, then the reactions (real, imagined, or anticipated) of significant other persons may form an essential part of the symptom, because these reactions are involved in the perceptual "feedback" concerned. Such a view enables us to understand, for example, why it is that hysterical symptoms may change with time. The role-response gained by virtue of a paralysed arm during World War I may, for example, only be obtained in later years by means of quite different symptoms or even character traits.

This point of view obliges us to make the assumption that the individual constantly scans his environment, in particular the reactions of others, in the process of unconscious symptom construction. The same holds true for the (often subtle) "transactions" that go on between people in ordinary social relations, in which there is a very rapid scanning of the responses of others to "trial" signals or behavioural indications of our own. Similarly, we respond, often quite unconsciously, to the signals inviting us to assume particular roles for others. If, based on such unconscious "scanning", "trials", and "signals", we find that the situation does not permit the gratification of an unconscious wishful phantasy through identity of perception, then we may discard a particular course of action (or seek other partners) in the attempt to attain unconscious wish-fulfilment.

Freud's masterly description of the "dream-work" needs, in the thesis expressed in this chapter, to be supplemented by an equal emphasis on the opposite, *centripetal* process of the dreamer perceiving the content of his dream and unconsciously translating it back into its latent meaning, so that wish-fulfilment is obtained by means of identity of perception. In a sense there is an unconscious "understanding-work" that goes in a parallel but opposite direction to the dream-work as described by Freud; and what is true of the dream can also be regarded as true for other "derivatives", for other surface expressions of unconscious wishes and phantasies. This allows us to add something further to the idea put forward previously that *all unconscious wish-fulfilment is brought about by some form of actualization.* The additional element is that *the perceived manifest actualization is unconsciously understood, and unconsciously translated back into its latent meaning.* In terms of the topographical model, this "decoding" and understanding would take place in the Preconscious system, while in the structural model it can be attributed to the unconscious ego. *Essential to the whole process is the need for consciousness to be protected from the knowledge of what is going on.*

In accordance with the thesis put forward here, such activities as sublimations can be regarded as symbolic actualizations that are *unconsciously understood* by the individual concerned. The person's consciousness is, at the same time, protected from awareness of the unconscious wishful phantasy being fulfilled. In short, if surgery—as is sometimes supposed—is a sublimation of sadistic wishes, then we would postulate that at some unconscious level the sadistic wishful phantasies are being gratified through a concealed identity of perception. The same would hold true for many character traits (see Chapter 5).

It is possible to take a further step in the argument presented here. If we can unconsciously "read", "decode", or "translate" the manifest derivatives of our own unconscious wishes and phantasies, then it seems likely that we have the capacity to understand, in a similar fashion, quite unconsciously, the latent meaning of much of what is produced by others, provided that there is sufficient background similarity between ourselves and the other person. Here again our own consciousness has to be protected, for we would surely be traumatically overwhelmed if we were to be consciously aware of the latent content of what is manifestly produced and communicated by others. It seems likely that unconscious communication of the latent content of thoughts, wishes, and phantasies goes on continually, and that this communication can occur because of the normal capacity to make an unconscious "good guess" in translating the meaning of the behaviour and communications of others of a similar cultural background. At the same time we normally defend ourselves strenuously against the awareness both of the existence of this unconscious communication and the content of what is communicated, although we occasionally allow unexplained "intuition" to come to consciousness. More frequently perhaps, we can permit ourselves to act on the unconscious information we gain about the latent meaning of other people's productions by making use of the mechanism of *rationalization*, a process by which we make our own apparently irrational behaviour, thoughts, and feelings appear plausible, if only to ourselves. In this context we can recall Freud's comment in "The Unconscious" that "It is a very remarkable thing that the *Ucs.* of one human being can react upon that of another, without passing through the *Cs.*". Skilled psychoanalysts have learned to make use of their own associations, self-observation, and self-analysis to gain some access to what has been unconsciously communicated to them. Unfortunately it is rather more difficult for us to gain similar access to what we unconsciously communicate to others, although analysts are increasingly aware of the intersubjective quality of their interaction with their patients.

CHAPTER THREE

On role-responsiveness

Introduction

In Chapter 2 Freud's notion of wish-fulfilment through the attainment of an identity of perception was described and amplified in general terms. In the present chapter it is applied specifically to countertransference and to the way in which pressures are placed upon the analyst to make him conform to an unconsciously wished-for role. The concepts of actualization and role-responsiveness are introduced, together with the idea of the "free-floating responsiveness" of the analyst in the analytic situation.

* * *

The term "countertransference" has many meanings, just as the term "transference" has. Freud first saw countertransference as referring to the analyst's blind spots that presented an obstacle to the analysis. From the beginning, countertransference was consistently seen as an obstruction to the freedom of the analyst's understanding of the patient. In this context, Freud regarded the analyst's mind as an "instrument", its effective functioning in the analytic situation being impeded by countertransference. Counter-transference in the analyst was equated with the resistance in the patient.[1]

As far as *transference* is concerned, it will be remembered that Freud saw it first as a hindrance but later regarded it as an indispensable vehicle for the analytic work. He did not, however, take a similar step for countertransference, and this inevitable development took place later. It was a crucial advance in psychoanalytic thinking when the countertransference

> began to be seen as a phenomenon of importance in helping the analyst to understand the hidden meaning of material brought by the patient. The essential idea . . . is that the analyst has elements of understanding and appreciation of the processes occurring in his patient, that these elements are not immediately conscious and that they can be discovered by the analyst if he monitors his own mental associations while listening to the patient.[2]

The first explicit statement of the *positive* value of countertransference was made by Heimann. Others have written on and developed the topic, but two papers by Heimann[3] have to be singled out as landmarks in the change of view regarding countertransference. She started by considering countertransference as referring to all the feelings that the analyst may experience towards his patient. Heimann remarks that the analyst has to be able "to *sustain* the feelings that are stirred up in him, as opposed to discharging them (as does the patient), in order to *subordinate* them to the analytic task in which he functions as the patient's mirror reflection". She assumes "that the analyst's unconscious understands that of his patient. This rapport on the deep level comes to the surface in the form of feelings which the analyst notices in response to his patient, in his 'countertransference'."[4]

There are many other important writings in this field, and they will not be commented on here, except to say that countertransference had been written about before Heimann's work. Heimann's contribution was to show clearly that the reaction of the analyst may usefully be the first clue to what is going on in the patient.

In *The Patient and the Analyst* the literature on transference was discussed in some detail, and it was concluded that transference need not be restricted to the illusory apperception of another person . . ., but can be taken to include the unconscious (and often subtle) attempts to manipulate or to provoke situations with others which are a concealed repetition of earlier experiences and relationships . . . when such transference manipulations or provocations occur in ordinary life, the person towards whom they are directed may either show that he does not accept the role, or may, if he is unconsciously disposed in that direction, in fact accept it, and act accordingly. It is likely that such acceptance or rejection of a transference role is not based on a conscious awareness of what is happening, but rather on unconscious cues. Transference elements enter to a varying degree into all relationships, and these (e.g. choice of spouse or employer) are often determined by some characteristic of the other person who (consciously or unconsciously) represents some attribute of an important figure of the past.

In the conclusions about transference the step was taken of extending the notion of the patient's *projection or externalization* of some aspect of the past (or of a figure of the past) onto the person of the analyst, to the patient's attempts to manipulate or to provoke situations with the analyst. Such "manipulations" are an important part of object relationships and enter in "trial" form into the "scanning" of objects in the process of object choice. In the transference, in many subtle ways, the patient attempts to prod the analyst into behaving in a particular way and unconsciously scans and adapts to his perception of the analyst's reaction (see the discussion of the search for an "identity of perception" in Chapter 2). The analyst, for his part, may be able to "hold" his response to this "prodding" in his consciousness as a reaction of his own that he perceives and attempts to contain, but there can be little doubt that there is a continual interaction occurring between the patient and the analyst on the non-verbal level as well as on a verbal basis. This allows us to think of the link between certain countertransference responses and the patient's transference via the overt or covert behavioural *interaction* between patient and analyst. So, although Heimann went so far as to point out that the analyst's response to the patient can be used as a basis for understanding the patient's material, often by thoughts and feelings that he can catch and hold in his awareness, this can be taken a little further.

No one can doubt the value of the analyst's continuing analysis of his countertransference. Interest in the subject has, in recent years, run parallel with an interest in the psychology of object relationships, and what is presented in the following is based on the assumption that a relationship—or, at the very least, an interaction—develops between the two parties to the analytic process. We are all aware of the special features of the analytic situation, with its capacity to induce the regressive revival of the past in the present, in a way that is usually entirely unconscious in, or rationalized by, the patient. On the other hand, we have the use made by the analyst of his special skills, including the employment by him of the capacity for free-floating attention, for self-analysis, and for the maintenance of what Winnicott[5] has called the "professional attitude". By free-floating attention is not meant the "clearing of the mind" of thoughts or memories, but, rather, the capacity to allow all sorts of thoughts, daydreams, and associations to enter the analyst's consciousness while he is simultaneously listening to and observing the patient.[6]

The interaction between the patient and the analyst is in large part (though, of course, not wholly) determined by what can be called the intrapsychic role-relationship that each party tries to impose on the other. One aspect of a role-relationship can be appropriate to the task in hand—that is, to the work of analysis. Certainly from the side of the *patient* we may see a whole variety of very specific role-relationships emerge. What should be emphasized is that the role-relationship of the patient in analysis at any particular time consists of a role in which he casts himself, and a *complementary* role in which he casts the analyst at that particular time. The patient's transference thus represents an attempt to gratify an unconscious wishful phantasy, involving representations in phantasy of his own self and that of the analyst, by trying to impose an interaction of a specific sort, an interrelationship (in the broadest sense of the word) between himself and the analyst. This is a very different view from the classical idea that transference is the patient's libidinal or aggressive energic cathexis of a past object being transferred to the image of the analyst in the present—a formulation that we, along with many others, believe to be inadequate. The patient's unconscious wishes and mechanisms with which we are concerned in our work are expressed intrapsychically in (descriptively) unconscious images or phantasies, in which both self and object in interaction have come to be represented in particular roles. These unconscious phantasies (preconscious in the topographical frame of reference[7]) are derived from and reflect the structured internal object relationships of the patient, a point that is developed in Chapter 8.

In a sense the patient attempts in the transference to actualize these in a disguised way, within the framework and limits of the analytic situation. In doing so, he resists becoming aware of any infantile relationship that he might be attempting to impose. It is worth underlining, at this point, the difference between the manifest content of what the patient brings and the latent unconscious content, in particular the infantile role-relationships reflected in unconscious transference phantasies, that he seeks to express or enact, *as well as the defensive role-relationships that he may have constructed.*

One could regard even the simplest instinctual wish as, from early in life, a wish to impose and to experience a *role-relationship* as a vehicle of instinctual gratification. However, what is said here applies not only to unconscious instinctual wishes, but to *the whole gamut of unconscious wishes related to all sorts of needs, gratifications, and defences.*

Parallel to the "free-floating attention" of the analyst is what can be called his *free-floating responsiveness.* The analyst is, of course, not a machine in absolute self-control, only experiencing on the one hand and delivering interpretations on the other, although some of the literature might seem to paint such a picture. Among many other things, he or she talks, greets the patient, arranges practical matters, and may joke and allow his responses to depart from the classical psychoanalytic norm to some extent. It is possible to say that in the analyst's overt reactions to the patient as well as in his thoughts and feelings, what can be called his "role-responsiveness" shows itself as a crucial element in his "useful" countertransference.

One or two examples from patients in analysis may illustrate what is meant. Their analyst (JS) writes

A patient, aged 35, had not had any previous analysis and had very little knowledge of the analytic process. He was referred to me because of extreme anxiety about making public presentations of his work, although he felt absolutely competent and at ease in private and informal discussions. He had had a very narrow education; he was the son of Eastern European immigrants, but because of his great financial and organizational skills had risen to a high position in an extremely large financial organization. In the initial interview it was found that he responded very well to trial interpretations, and I felt that work with him was going to be rewarding and a pleasure. During the first week or two of his analysis I found that I was talking very much more than I usually do. I should say that I am not an unduly silent analyst. After a little while I felt that something was making me anxious with regard to this patient, and some self-analytic reflection on my part showed me that I was afraid that he would leave, that I was anxious to keep him, to lower his anxiety level so that he would stay in analysis, and that I was talking more than usual to avoid the aggressive side of his ambivalent feelings. When I saw this, I felt relieved and reverted to my usual analytic behaviour. However, I noticed at once the urge to talk during the session and became aware that the patient, by a slight inflection of his voice, succeeded in ending every sentence with an interrogation, although he did not usually formulate a direct question. This gave me the opportunity to point out to him what he was doing (he was quite unaware of it, just as I had been unaware of it in him) and to show him how much he needed to have me reassure him by talking. He then recalled how he would feel extremely anxious as a child when his father returned home from work, and he would compulsively engage his father in conversation, asking him many questions, to be reassured that his father was not angry with him. His father had been a professional fighter, was very violent, and the patient was terrified of him but needed his father's admiration and love—to be the preferred child. (Later in the analysis we were to see, as one might expect, his fear of his own hostility to his father.) He told me that his father had the habit of not listening and not responding, and how frightening this was. The patient then realized that from early childhood onwards he had developed the trick of asking questions without directly asking them, and we could conclude that this had become part of his character, being intensified in situations where he feared disapproval and needed supplies of reassurance from authority figures.

The point made here is that, apart from the "ordinary" elements in his analytic work, the analyst will often respond overtly to the patient in a way that he feels indicates *only* his own (the analyst's) problems, his own blind spots, and he may successfully resort to self-analysis to discover the pathology behind his particular response or attitude to the patient. However, it seems likely that very often the irrational response of the analyst, which his professional conscience leads him to see entirely as a blind spot of his own, may be usefully regarded as a compromise formation between his own tendencies and *his reflexive acceptance of the role that the patient is forcing on him*.

Naturally, some analysts will be more susceptible to certain roles than others, and the proportion of the contribution from the side of the patient and from the side of the analyst will vary greatly from one instance to another. Not all the irrational actions and reactions of the analyst are reflections of the role into which he is manoeuvred by the patient. What is suggested with regard to this example is simply how the patient, by a subtle element in his behaviour, evoked an overt response from the analyst that had, at first sight, seemed *only* irrational countertransference. It is worth commenting that the view being taken here does not in any way support the view that all countertransference responses are due to what the patient has imposed on the analyst.

A further example follows. This relates to a patient in her late twenties, a schoolteacher. The analyst (JS) reports that the patient

came to treatment because of social and sexual difficulties, and after some time it became clear that she was terrified of her penis-envy and of her hostility towards her mother, had multiple phobic anxieties and needed, mainly through intellectualization and organizational control of others, including in her teaching, to "structure" her world so that she always knew exactly "where she was". Her need to do this emerged in the transference, and after two and a half years of analytic work her psychopathology had become very much clearer and she was much improved and happier. However, there was one strand of material that had remained obscure. From the beginning she had cried during each session, and I had routinely passed her the box of tissues whenever she began to cry. Now I did not know why I did this but, having begun the practice, I did not feel inclined to change it without some good reason. Without knowing why, I had not felt it appropriate to take up her failure to bring her own tissues or a handkerchief, although with other patients I would have done this. There were many determinants of her crying, including her mourning for the mother she wanted to kill off, for the father she felt she had to give up, and so on.

It transpired that when she was about two years old, a second child, a brother, had been born, and she felt that she had lost her mother's attention; she remembered that at about two and a half years of age she was relegated to playing on her own in the back-yard while her brother was being washed and changed. At this time she had also been sent to a kindergarten, and she had the memory of being very withdrawn and climbing into the rabbit hutch at the nursery school and cuddling a white rabbit. She then told me that she had later learned that after a short while at this school she had been diagnosed as "autistic" by the school psychologist, being apparently very regressed, with uncontrollable rages and tantrums.

By this point in her analysis we were able to get at the repetition in the present of her fear of soiling and disgracing herself, and her need to control her objects as she had to control her sphincters. However, there was clearly something that was an important unconscious phantasy for her, which had not been elicited. I had the feeling that we were "stuck" in the analytic work. One day something unusual happened in the analysis. She had begun to cry silently, but this time I failed to respond, and she suddenly began to upbraid me and criticize me for not passing her the tissues. She became quite panicky and began to accuse me of being callous and uncaring. I responded by saying that I did not know why I had not passed her the tissues at that particular point, but if she could go on talking perhaps we could both understand more about it. What emerged then was material that lent much specificity to something that we had not been able to crystallize previously. It became clear that her great need for control and for "structures" in her life was based not on a fear of soiling herself, but, rather, on a fear that she would soil or wet herself *and that there would not be an adult around to clean her up.* This turned out to be the fear that dominated her life. It was a specific phantasy that seemed to have been elaborated during the late anal phase, under the impact of the mother's withdrawal from her because of the birth of the second child. The discovery and working through of this specific phantasy marked a crucial point in her analysis. I do not want to go into any more detail about her material, except to say that I think that I must have picked up unconscious cues from the patient that prompted me to behave in a certain way in her analysis—both to keep passing her the tissues and then to omit doing so. (It would be pure speculation to link the two and a half years of analysis with the age when her anxiety started.) I believe that this patient had forced me into a role, quite unconsciously on her part and on mine—a role corresponding to that of a parental introject, in which I enacted the part, first of the attentive mother and then suddenly that of the parent who did not clean her up. In the session I was not around to make sure that she was clean, just as she felt that, with the birth of her brother, her mother had not been around to clean her, being busy paying attention to the new baby.

It has been suggested that the analyst has, within certain limits, a free-floating behavioural responsiveness in addition to his free-floating conscious attention. Within the limits set by the analytic situation he will, unless he becomes aware of it, tend to comply with the role demanded of him, to integrate it into his mode of responding and relating to the patient. He can often catch this counter-response in himself, particularly if it is in the direction of being inappropriate. However, he may only become aware of it through observing his own behaviour, responses, and attitudes *after these have been carried over into action.* What this chapter has been concerned with is the special case of the analyst regarding some aspect of his own behaviour as deriving entirely from within himself when it could more usefully be seen as a *compromise* between his own tendencies or propensities and the role-relationship in unconscious phantasy (i.e. the phantasy derivative of a structured internal self–object relationship) that the patient is unconsciously seeking to establish.

Although the terms "projection", "putting parts of oneself into another", and "externalization" are useful, they give a one-sided view of the interaction between two people. While the Kleinian concept of projective identification has taken the psychoanalytic model, particularly the clinical model, a major step forward, it is often used too broadly and indiscriminately, and its precise meaning needs to be specified whenever it is applied. The problem of what is meant by projective identification has been discussed in detail elsewhere.[8]

In the years since the publication of the paper on which this chapter is based,[9] psychoanalysis has seen the development of a "constructivist" approach, in which the analytic process is seen as being jointly and continuously constructed by both patient and analyst. (In recent years a significant number of authors have stressed and developed the view that the analyst always takes part in determining the transference.) Certainly there is truth in what the constructivists have to say, and we can regard their position as one that will have an important influence on our understanding of patient–analyst interaction, for it is certainly the case that the interaction between two persons can be seen in the processes of dynamic exchange that characterize transference and countertransference, where a complicated system of unconscious cues, both given and received, is involved. Such an exchange of cues occurs, not only in the aspects of transference and countertransference discussed here, but in normal object relationships and in the process of temporary or permanent object choice as well.

CHAPTER FOUR

On object relations
and affects

Introduction

This chapter is about the development of object relationships, with special reference to the role of affect in that development. The topic is not an easy one to discuss because the psychoanalytic theory of object relationships is far from satisfactory, and our theory of affect is, at best, in a state of healthy and constructive chaos. When we think about object relationships, we have to cope in our minds with such concepts as relationships to part and whole objects, to objects that are need-satisfying as opposed to those that possess object-constancy. We have objects to whom there is an anaclitic relationship, towards whom we are ambivalent, who are narcissistic objects, selfobjects, or simply good or bad objects. There are objects with whom we have sado-masochistic relationships; objects biological and objects psychological; and many others. In the face of all this, we have found it increasingly necessary to ask ourselves how the theory of object relationships can be integrated into our psychoanalytic psychology. The answer lies, we believe, in the application of the ideas put forward in Chapters 2 and 3, and in propositions that follow regarding the role of feeling states in the psychoanalytic theory of mental functioning.

* * *

It was appropriate, for some considerable time during the development of psychoanalytic theory, to regard an object relationship as the "cathexis of an object" with libidinal (and later with aggressive) energy. This is a way of saying, within an "energy" frame of reference, that an object relationship is the state of loving, hating, or both loving and hating another person or an aspect of that person. But it is increasingly clear that conceiving of an object relationship as the energic investment of an object is inadequate and simplistic.[1] We know, for example, that object relationships are two-sided, that in their development they involve activity on the part of the other person (for example, the caretaking mother). We also know that our thoughts and feelings about the important objects in our lives, our behaviour towards them and our expectations of them, are extremely complex. This begins with the intricate interaction between the child and his biological objects in the earliest weeks and months of life. Phenomena such as these have been studied outside the treatment situation by psychoanalytic child observers such as René Spitz,[2] Donald Winnicott,[3] Margaret Mahler and her colleagues,[4] and Bowlby,[5] as well as by many experimenters working in a systematic way more recently on the reaction of very young infants to the different people in their environments.[6] On the basis of theoretical reconstructions from analytic material, some analysts (notably Melanie Klein and her followers) have stressed the complexity of early object relationships.[7] Unfortunately in their formulations they appear to have attributed profound psychological knowledge to the infant by confounding psychological and biological behaviour. Consequently, they endow the infant with psychological intentionality and complex cognition in the first weeks of life. In our view, the infant is probably, for a considerable time and to a significant extent, the passive observer and experiencer of his own activities, feelings, and sensations. The capacity to create and manipulate phantasies and thoughts in an active fashion will, in our view, occur well after the first months of life.

As indicated in Chapter 3, the relationship between two people, even if looked at from only one side in terms of the subjective experience and activities of *one* of the people concerned, involves very subtle and complicated cues and signs. There are unconscious exchanges of messages, as well as the conscious or unconscious experiencing of all sorts of other interactions. Each partner, at any given moment, has a role for the other and negotiates with the other to get him or her to respond in a particular way. A whole variety of feelings, wishes, thoughts, and expectations are involved in the interaction that is characteristic of the ongoing relationship between two people. This is true not only for a relationship between two real people: an object relationship *in phantasy* will also involve a similar sort of interaction between self- and object-representations, except that in a phantasy relationship the person having the phantasy can control the relationship represented in it in a wish-fulfilling way to a much greater degree than he can in real life.

Throughout, it has been clear that we regard the question of wish-fulfilment and gratification as extremely important with regard to object relationships and to object relations theory. As Kernberg remarked in *Internal World and External Reality*,[8]

> Psychoanalytic object relations theory . . . is not an additional metapsychological viewpoint, nor is it opposed to the structural, development-genetic, dynamic, economic and adaptive viewpoints; rather it represents a special approach or focus within the structural viewpoint that links structure more closely with developmental, genetic, and dynamic aspects of mental functioning; it occupies an intermediary realm between psychoanalytic metapsychology, on the one hand, and direct clinical formulations in the psychoanalytic situation, on the other.

It is worth reiterating that in this context wish-fulfilment is a far broader concept than that of the gratification of instinctual drives or their derivatives, or the obtaining of instinctual "discharge".[9] We can assume that what we call object relationships in this chapter (in the special sense of internal role relationships) are linked to and represent the fulfilment of important needs in the developing child, as well as in the adolescent and adult. Such needs may show themselves as wishes, which may or may not be predominantly instinctual. Although the term "need" is used here, we are not referring only to needs in the sense of the primitive biologically based needs of the infant. The view that all relationships fulfil needs is not the same as equating them with the so-called "need-satisfying" (or "part-object") relationships of the infant or young child; nor is "need" the same as "instinctual drive" in this context. After object constancy[10] has been reached by the child, the constant attachment to and affection for the object represent the fulfilment of very special secondary needs that have developed in the individual (that is, needs that are satisfied by interacting with the unique object in a particular way). Valuing the relationship with an object comes to be represented, of course, as valuing the object; and concern for the relationship soon becomes concern for the object.

In Chapter 3 it is pointed out that a great many wishes arise as a result of forces that are not instinctual, and that wishes can be stimulated by factors in the external world as well as by internal sources of affective disequilibrium. The common motivational pathway for all such stimuli, whatever their origin, is the change brought about in the individual's conscious or unconscious affective state.

We have spoken of the various needs—instinctually driven or otherwise—of the individual, including all those needs that arise from disturbances of his internal psychic equilibrium, and of the wishes that develop in association with these needs. To this we have to add something extremely important. The individual is constantly obtaining a special form of gratification through his interaction with his environment and with his own self (Chapter 6), constantly providing himself with a sort of nourishment, something that we can call "affirmation". Through his interaction with different aspects of his world, in particular his objects, he gains a variety of reassuring feelings. This need for "nourishment", for affirmation and reassurance, has to be satisfied constantly, to yield a background of safety[11] and—as far as possible—well-being. We usually see such needs only when their satisfaction is obstructed in some way, as when a small child playing happily suddenly loses sight of its mother and becomes distressed.[12] The wish to interact with mother will be intense and will have a very definite content. Here we can see that this sort of object relationship is based on a continual wish-fulfilment, the wish being to obtain reassurance (and the resulting feeling of safety) that the mother is nearby. Of course, affirmation from the object can be gained even when the object is experienced as a harsh and punitive one, because feelings of safety are gained through the perception of the familiar, even though that familiar perception is unpleasant. The need for affirmation by the object is at its highest when the child's attitude to the object is an ambivalent one, as it naturally is during certain phases of development. The greater the hostile component of the ambivalence, the more dependent the child will become on gaining reassurance from the object. Later in life, the child (and adult) will increasingly be able to make use of an unconscious dialogue with his objects in phantasy in order to gain reassurance. The need for affirmation, even though that affirmation is embedded in painful feelings, is at the root of our attachment to our superego introjects[13]—indeed, to our internal objects in general.

It should be noted that, in what follows, affects are looked at entirely as subjective experiences. They are regarded as feeling states that may be pleasurable or unpleasurable. Such feeling states may be within conscious awareness or outside it. This view of affect has been elaborated elsewhere.[14] If we can allow ourselves to depart from the view that all unconscious wishes are motivated solely by instinctual drives, we can then concede that (just like the need for pleasure) anxiety or any other painful feeling can mobilize a wish—for example, a wish to run away, to escape an external danger situation. However, although at one time such wishes may be acceptable to us, during development they may become unacceptable and remain as urgent but unconscious wishful impulses that are defended against.

Wishes that represent past solutions and adaptations, particularly childhood ones, constantly recur but may be kept back because they are no longer acceptable, because they arouse conflict. They are defended against when our feelings of security or safety are threatened, as they constantly are. Nevertheless, although such wishes are not felt to be appropriate or acceptable in the present, they persist.[15] We integrate these past wishes, as they re-emerge in the present, with new ones formed because of socialization and other factors.

The way in which we gratify or fulfil unconscious wishes of all sorts may be extremely subtle and disguised because of the need to protect consciousness from directly experiencing the "unaccept-able" content of the unconscious wish. Although our behaviour does not consist only in repeating past object relations, it is true that much of our life is involved in the concealed repetition of internalized early object relationships in one form or another. This includes those patterns of relationship that have developed as safety-giving or anxiety-reducing manoeuvres, as well as those that satisfy instinctual wishes. Much of what we call illness, in-cluding occasionally quite severe psychological illness, may be looked at from this standpoint. All the defensive displacements, reversals, and other forms of disguise can enter into the way in which we repeat or attempt to repeat wish-fulfilling early relation-ships. At this point it would be useful to give a simple example of the relation between early object relationships and wish-fulfilment as shown in an adult patient.[16]

This patient, in his late thirties, is a practising homosexual with what might be called a narcissistic character disorder. He also tends to be hypochondriacal, and at a certain point in his analysis developed an itch that he believed (and managed to persuade his physician to believe) was due to scabies. He was given some ointment, with detailed instruction about its application, and arranged for his boyfriend to wake him in the middle of the night to apply the ointment to his body. After two days the itch disappeared, but a week later he began to itch again and consulted his physician. By this time the doctor had doubts about whether he had scabies, but he was prescribed the same treatment and made the same arrangement with his companion. However, when it happened again, his physician concluded that he had a neurodermatitis of some sort, and even hinted to him that he might be suffering from a psycho-genic itch.

In the analysis it was clear that he had a very strong wish that his analyst should be the one who would apply the medication, and this could be interpreted to him. He then recalled that he had suffered from eczema as a baby and that he regularly woke at night because of his discomfort. He would call for his mother, who would come to him and put a soothing lotion all over his body. This was, of course, very erotic for him, but the erotic element only served to reinforce the link to his mother and his need to feel her close and soothing presence. He later developed, as many such children do, extreme separation anxiety, and at night would call for his mother who came to comfort him, even though he did not always have a physical itch, but instead expressed a fear or worry of one sort or another. When a younger brother was born (the patient was five years old) he could get his mother to come to him every night on some sort of pretext.

In this patient, the wish to get close to mother, especially when he was anxious, showed itself, not simply in the quite gross symptom of the itching skin, but also in a personality style in which he would constantly have problems that would worry him, urgent questions that would have to be answered. It was possible to see that much of his character was built on his need to have constant "itches" of one sort or another. He would actively create the "itches", particularly when everything was going well. This entered into the transference, but, curiously, the analyst's countertransference response was that he felt that he wanted to help the patient over any immediate problem the patient might have. The analyst was being tempted to play the role of the comforting mother. This was wished for by the patient to recreate the feeling (and to gratify the wishful unconscious phantasy) of the presence of the mother. This wish to re-experience the mother's presence took a variety of forms and could be seen in many areas of the patient's life. This aspect of the patient's behaviour and character can be seen both as a disguised form of wish-fulfilment and as the repetition of an object relationship, as it manifests itself as an unconscious phantasy in the "here-and-now". There are, of course, other clinical points that can be discussed about the patient (such as his fear of women, his defences against his aggression, and so on). These are not relevant to this presentation, but one could comment on the possibility that the patient's mother needed, for her own purposes, to have her child dependent on her—that is, that she probably needed a particular role-response from him that he, in turn, provided, in order to feel safe and secure with her. There are occasions when it is clinically important to verbalize such a reconstruction to the patient.

It is appropriate to remind ourselves that, in psychological terms, every wish involves a self-representation, an object-representation, and a representation of the interaction between these. There is a role for both self and object. It has been pointed out how relevant this is for an understanding of transference and for those aspects of countertransference referred to as role-responsiveness, which occurs outside the analysis as well as in it. A person manipulated in this way may reject or ignore the role, may defend against it, or may accept it—or part of it. While transference elements are present in all relationships, what is also necessary for a real relationship of any significance to be established is the propensity of the second person, towards whom the transference is directed, to react in a special way. In the process of object-choice the other person is subtly tested to see whether or not he or she will respond in a particular way. The idea of "testing out" the role-responsiveness of another person brings together the concepts of object choice and object relationship, inasmuch as we commonly make rapid trial relationships until we find someone who fits the role we want the "other" to play and who is prepared to allow himself to respond according to that role.*

Not only do the ideas of object choice and object relationship come together if we think in terms of the individual seeking particular role relationships (in the transference or outside it in his everyday life), but the traditional distinction between the search for objects on the one hand and the search for wish-fulfilment or need-satisfaction on the other also fades into insignificance. *The two can be regarded as essentially the same.* If a person creates stable object relationships, then he creates, through his interaction with his objects, through their mutual affectively significant communication, both a constantly recurring source of wish-fulfilment and a constant object relationship.

Clinical experience shows that an object relationship may have a very definite pattern, a time sequence, inherent in it. We all know of cases in which someone gets on well with an employer or a

---

*The term "role" as used here refers to an expected or wished-for pattern of psychosocial reaction and behaviour. It does not refer to "role-playing" of the theatrical variety but is used in its accepted sociological or socio-psychological sense.

lover, and after some weeks or months a sudden disappointment or disillusionment occurs. In analysis this can often be traced either to an adaptive pattern of relationship from childhood or to a defence against dangerous closeness. The important point here is that the relationship has a temporal dimension. There is a script for the dialogue.

We have put forward the view that the patient in analysis attempts to *actualize* the particular role relationship embodied in his current dominant unconscious wish or phantasy, and that he will try to do this (usually in a disguised and symbolic way) within the framework of the psychoanalytic situation. People also do this outside analysis, and it is not a great step to say that *the striving towards actualization is part of the wish-fulfilling aspect of all object relationships*. In discussing this topic in Chapter 3 it was pointed out that the analyst not only makes use of his free-floating attention, but also has what can be called a free-floating *responsiveness* to the patient and will often, to a certain degree, allow himself to go along with (or defend against) the role that the patient imposes or attempts to impose on him. The analyst usually sets certain limits to what he will allow himself to do. Some analysts will have wider limits in one case than in another, or may even comply completely with the roles unconsciously demanded of them. When this happens, the analyst will often see himself behaving (or feel tempted to behave) in an apparently irrational way, which he finds, via his self-analysis, to be apparently neurotic; and yet he has responded to the patient in that particular way because the patient has, in a sense, "pressed the right buttons" in him. Although the analyst may have a propensity of his own to function in this way, his reaction may represent *his compliance with the role that the patient wants him to play*. Sometimes we only get the useful information that this can provide after we have, for example, noticed a departure from our usual way of dealing with the patient. These enactments, or *role-evocations*, can provide useful information to the analyst about the wish-fulfilling object relationship that the patient is unconsciously trying to actualize in the transference. Of course, not all irrational behaviour of the analyst should be regarded as a role-response to the patient, but much of it is.

In Chapter 2 wish-fulfilment occurring through actualization was studied in relation to dreams, where unconscious wish-fulfilment is obtained through hallucinatory actualization, conscious-ness being "deceived" about what is occurring. It was postulated that there is also an "understanding-work" that parallels the "dream-work" described by Freud. This understanding-work is part of the perception of the dream, so that the dream content is unconsciously understood as a wish-fulfilment. The aim of the dream-work is to protect consciousness at all costs, but an essential function of the dream is that it has to be *experienced as reality* at the time of the dream in order for it to be a wish-fulfilment. Moreover, it is *experienced* as a wish-fulfilment, and this process of under-standing occurs unconsciously. It is clear that we cannot confine ourselves to the view that simple surface expression in disguised form serves, on its own, to gratify an unconscious wish. This view is a relic of the idea that gratification of unconscious wishes takes place by means of a centrifugal "discharge" of energy.* If we make use of the idea that wish-fulfilment comes about through reaching an "identity of perception", then the dream needs to be uncon-sciously perceived and understood by the dreamer.

The understanding-work referred to applies not only to dreams, but to many other forms of actualization as well. We can think here of hallucinatory and delusional actualization, actualiza-tion through illusional perception, symbolic actualization, actuali-zation by means of modifying one's own behaviour or through modification of the external world, and so on. Actualization through conscious daydreams may be satisfying, to the degree to which the feeling of unreality of the daydream can be suspended. We have seen previously that the wish contains the representation of a role relationship, an affectively invested dialogue between self and object, with both playing a part. Consequently, to the extent that the wish contains an object relationship, every form of actuali-zation will represent the fulfilment of a wished-for relationship. Thus, in our real relationships with others, in our phantasies, in our artistic productions, in our symptoms, in our dreams, in our play,

---

* The idea that wish-fulfilment occurs through obtaining an "identity of perception" is not compatible with the notion of wish-fulfilment through the discharge of instinctual drive energy. It was probably this incompatibility that caused Freud to neglect the concept of identity of perception after he had put it forward in *The Interpretation of Dreams*.

and perhaps even in our scientific productions, we may actualize unconscious wishful internal object relationships in a symbolic form. This point may be usefully illustrated by an example.

Mr P., a successful scientist, came for analysis because (among other things) he had a severe work problem. He could, in fact, produce the work required of him and had made several notable contributions in his field. He had previously had analysis for some years, and at the beginning of his current analysis it seemed that all the well-known factors causing a work difficulty of the sort he had were present. His need to delay getting down to work until the very last minute appeared to be an oedipal problem, in which he could not allow himself to feel that he had satisfied oedipal sexual and aggressive wishes by working well. It was also seen to be part of an anal retentive tendency, which had persisted for most of his life. Analysis of his fear of success, of his need to hold on until the last moment, and of many other elements that were related to his work problems did not do much to give him greater insight, although all of this material emerged in the transference and was taken up in transference terms; but his problems remained. Eventually, through the analyst's awareness of his countertransference response to the way in which the patient could not come to the point in giving an account of what had happened to him the previous day, the significant function of his symptom (one might even call it a character trait) became clear. By allowing himself to get into a state of anxiety and by creating a feeling of great internal pressure as time passed and his work was not done, he could recreate, to a degree that was almost hallucinatory in intensity, the feeling of being nagged and even screamed at by his mother. It became clear that he used his symptom to re-experience an object relationship, one in which a wished-for sado-masochistic relationship with the mother was actualized. However, what was present was more than the simple sexualization of anxiety: it was a real need to feel secure by re-experiencing the earlier relationship to the mother, though he had to pay a painful price for this. It also emerged that his constant battle with his mother was a reflection of the way in which he had coped, as a toddler, with many blows to his self-esteem and omnipotence. It seemed that he could become "important" by being provocative, and that his mother played in with this to a remarkable degree.

There is no doubt of the importance to us of an understanding of the ways in which individuals actualize the infantile object relationships present in their unconscious phantasies through many different activities in their daily lives. These activities may show themselves in relation to other people, or may simply be present as so-called "character traits". Some character traits are specifically designed to evoke particular responses in others, and this may give us an additional avenue of approach to the understanding of character (see Chapter 5).

In all of this there is the implication that we can consider interpersonal relationships within the framework of our intrapsychic psychoanalytic psychology, by taking into account the various hidden ways in which people attempt to actualize their conscious and unconscious wishes and the object relationships reflected in the individual's wishful phantasies. Members of a group will "negotiate" with one another in terms of the responses that each needs and those that are demanded of them. The members of the group may even make unconscious "deals" or "transactions" in terms of the responses involved, so that each gains as much object-related wish-fulfilment as possible in return for concessions to other members of the group.

Let us sum up the views that have been put forward so far. The internal object relationship can be conceived of as an intrapsychic relationship, depicted via derivatives—that is, those mental representations that form an intrinsic part of the unsatisfied wish or of the wishful phantasy. After a certain point in the child's development we cannot speak of a wish that does not have ideational content; and the ideational content of a wishful phantasy is, in the context of our work as psychoanalysts, very often centred around the patient's representation of himself in interaction with the analyst. *The object plays as important a role as the self in the mental representation that is part of the wish.* We are constantly motivated to replenish a feeling of security, well-being, or affirmation, to gain the nutriment or aliment needed to feel "good", to maintain a basic feeling of security and integrity; and we do this almost automatically via a dialogue with our objects in reality or in phantasy. If we see object relationships as wish-fulfilments in a broad sense, then the fulfilment of the wished-for object relationship comes about through the finding of an object (in reality, in phantasy, or in both) that will act and react in the appropriate way. Just as the dream provides an identity of perception, so does the experience of the real or imagined object relationship provide an identity of perception—indeed, an identity of relation—in satisfying the wish. As in the dream and in other derivatives of unconscious wishes, the mental apparatus may find very roundabout routes to obtaining wish-fulfilment (and thus actualize a wished-for object relationship) through a disguised identity of perception.

If we turn now to the question of the *development* of object relationships, we can further assume that significant relationships begin to be built up in the mind of the child very early in life. We can assume that the infant is an *experiencing* animal, at the very least from birth, that it has a sensorium that is affected by stimuli from within (especially those arising from biological needs and instinctual drives) and by stimuli from without, of particular significance being those arising from the actions and attitudes of the mother. The infant equally affects the caretaker, and this subject has been studied in great detail.[17] It is our assumption that the subjective experiences that register on the infant's sensorium are, in the first instance, predominantly feeling states, although these are mixed with other sensations as well. The laying down of memory-traces and the organization of perceptual and memory structures gradually leads to further development of the infant's representational world,[18] which acts as a basis for the progressive organization of the child's subjective experiences and motor activities. Naturally the *particular* interaction that he has with the external world and his particular individual capacities will exercise a profound influence on the development of the child's representational world. During his early development he will create representations of his own self and of his objects, and later he will develop symbolic representations for use in thought and phantasy.

In the development of object relationships (that is, of structured role relationships), the part played by affective experience is central. *A subjective experience only has or retains meaning for the child if it is linked with feeling.* The assumption is made that ultimately all meaning is developmentally and functionally related to states of feeling, and that an experience that does not have some relation to a feeling state has no psychological significance for the individual at all. This is in line with a view previously put forward on the role of feelings as psychic regulators—namely, that "the ultimate guiding or regulatory principle in adaptation from a psychological point of view relates to feeling states of one form or another and that to equate these with energic equilibrium and with drive equilibrium in particular may be misleading or incorrect."[19]

We can speculate that, at first, the child will have two great classes of subjective experience—those experiences that are pleasant, gratifying, comfortable, and associated with safety on the one hand, and those that are unpleasant, uncomfortable, and painful, on the other. The child naturally reacts in different ways to experiences that are either pleasurable or unpleasurable. If he is confronted with a situation that he perceives, in his own primitive way, as one associated with pleasant feelings, he will respond to it by joyful gurgling and other signs of happiness. If he is subjected to a situation that is painful or unpleasant in some other way, he may become alert but, equally, may withdraw, showing a response of distress in one form or another. If we speak only in terms of recognition rather than of remembering, we could postulate that the first important distinction *recognized* by the child in the world of his experience is the difference between the two basic classes of affects, of feeling-experiences. Both are reacted to when they impinge on the child, but in different and opposing ways. If we stretch the idea of "object" a little further than usual, we could say that the first objects of the child are the experiences of pleasure and satisfaction on the one hand and those of unpleasure and pain on the other. In a sense we could say that from very early on the child begins to experience a dialogue with these primary objects, although at first he may have no control over the dialogue.

Let us put it another way: pleasure is greeted by the child with joy and excitement, and the child will welcome it. Unpleasure, on the other hand, is greeted with primitive mechanisms of rejection, avoidance, and withdrawal, by anger and even rage. These initial differentiated responses to the two major classes of experience, the two primary "objects" of the child, are, in the beginning, biologically based. They are not under the (conscious or unconscious) voluntary control of the infant, although his responses immediately affect the state of his sensorium. This leads very quickly to the development and construction of further mental representations that become linked with the different feeling states. With further development subcategories of each affective class will be recognized, as will compounds of different feelings.

Thus the first division of the child's subjective experiential world can be regarded as the division into pleasure and unpleasure *per se* as objects. Because the child is in constant psychobiologically based interaction with his environment and constantly receives feedback from that environment, a feedback that is intimately associated with feelings of one sort or another, he will attempt to maintain his relationship to the "nice" or "good" object as much as possible and to minimize, to the extent that he can, his contact with the "nasty" or "bad" object. The "objects" referred to here are initially constellations of subjective experience in which "self" and "not-self" have not yet been differentiated. These primary "affective objects" are relatively chaotic masses of pleasurable feelings and sensations on the one hand and unpleasurable ones on the other.

All of this forces the infant into a dialogue with his subjective experiences (see Chapter 6), though the boundaries between himself and others have not yet been subjectively created. It is worth noting that evidence from the so-called "baby-watchers" may appear to contradict this,[20] in that the child does seem to have an innate, "given" tendency to relate to objects. However, we do not perceive a contradiction in this, in that we are referring here to *subjective* experiences, not to overt behaviour. The distinction between the "experiential" and "non-experiential" realms of mental functioning is relevant here.

The realm of subjective experience (in German *Erlebnis* but not *Erfahrung*) refers to the experience of the phenomenal content of wishes, impulses, memories, phantasies, sensations, percepts, feelings, and the like. All we "know", we know only through such subjective phenomenal representations, which may vary widely in content, quality and intensity.

Having said this, we would add immediately that experiential content of any sort *can be either conscious or unconscious.*

Implicit in this is the view that the individual may "know" his own experiential content outside consciousness, that ideas can be experienced and feelings felt outside conscious awareness; and that he does not know that he unconsciously "knows". . . . In sharp contrast is the "non-experiential realm." This is the realm of forces and energies, of mechanisms and apparatuses; of organised structures, both biological and psychological; of sense organs and means of discharge. The non-experiential realm is intrinsically unknowable, except insofar as it can become known through the creation or occurrence of a phenomenal event in the realm of subjective experience.[21]

As other sensory and perceptual subjective experiences become associated with the primary "affective objects", we begin to get the formation of increasingly complex representations of objects in the sense of people or parts of people. This occurs in both the non-experiential and the experiential realms and includes the infant's own self-representation. There seems an increasing amount of evidence that there is a given, inborn basis for the child's early responses to external objects, although there is no evidence that the child subjectively "knows" the difference between "internal" and "external", a distinction that he may appear to show in his *behaviour* in interaction with others on the basis of built-in "wiring". We can assume that there are early predispositions based on inborn organized perceptual and response tendencies related to *potential* object-representations, just as there is evidence to postulate an inborn neurological substratum for the body schema or body image.[22] Newson and Newson[23] have described how the child only achieves a fully articulated knowledge of his world as he becomes involved in social transactions with other communicating human beings. It has been shown[24] that the infant can manifest extremely complicated behavioural responses to external events and circumstances, and that eye, hand, and arm co-ordination exists early to a greater degree than we would expect, even from the first weeks of life. Of greatest significance in all the studies of infant interaction with things and persons in their environment is the very young infant's dependence on experiencing appropriate sensorial and affective feedback. This applies not only to such ordinary things as reaching and grasping but *par excellence* to social interactions. We cannot go into an account of the recent work in this fascinating area, but there are excellent summaries elsewhere. However, we would like to echo the words of Newson and Newson[25] who say:

> Clearly, findings of this kind ... suggest that infants at birth are already possessed of the necessary sensory, motor and neural equipment to make it possible for them to respond appropriately towards real objects in a three dimensional world. ... *At the same time we need to treat with caution the suggestion ... that the human infant is somehow inherently possessed of the "knowledge" that seen objects are tangible.* Behaviour, however complicated, carries no necessary implication that the organism is capable of appreciating the ends towards which its own behaviour is directed. ... However accurately a guided missile is able to seek out its target, we do not generally feel it necessary to credit the missile with having *knowledge* about the target. [italics added]

Experimental work[26] has shown that the face of his mother fascinates the infant almost from birth, and slowed-down video-recordings of an interacting mother–baby pair show that the different sensori-motor components of the infant's and the mother's activities are highly synchronized and that the infant's action sequences are organized so that they "mesh", with a high degree of precision, with patterns of action produced by the caretaker. As Newson and Newson[27] put it:

> The fact is that, from a very early age indeed, infants appear to be capable of taking part in dialogue-like exchanges with other human beings. Thus, when the adult talks to the infant, he displays all the complex gestural accompaniments that one normally expects of attentive listening: and when the adult pauses, the infant can reply with a fully articulated, gesturally animated, conversation-like response. Trevarthen and his colleagues have described the complex coordinated interaction between infant and caretaker as an "innate intersubjectivity".

After the formation of the child's "primary affective objects", his innate predispositions and his experience (including his awareness of his own responses, in a primitive way, *after* they have occurred and of his social experience in the interaction with his mother) will lead him gradually to construct a further boundary. This is the boundary between his representation of his self and the representations of his objects (primarily of the caretaking mother). In addition, he will create increasingly complex representations of the interactions, the relationships, the dialogues between himself and his objects. All these representations will be intimately linked with feeling states of one sort or another, even if the associated feelings are reduced to a signal.*

The essential motivating forces prompting both ego development and the interrelated development of object relationships ultimately derive, in our view, from the changes in the subject's affective experience, from changes in his relation to his primary affective objects. The economics involved are the economics of affective experiences, both pleasant and unpleasant. To put it another way: from earliest infancy, the individual attempts to maintain his close, joyous, and blissful relationship to the basic "good" feeling state, to a constellation of pleasure, well-being, and feelings of safety. Simultaneously, he will attempt to obliterate from his experience the other major primary "affective object"— that is, unpleasure and pain. Incidentally, this raises an interesting point, for we would take the view that the child does not initially try to get rid of feelings of unpleasure by projecting them into an object in the "external" world, but that the child tries to make them *disappear*. The simplest form of this is the infant's turning away of his head when confronted with an object, the perception of whom is associated with unpleasant feelings.

In this context one could paraphrase Freud's remarks in his paper "On Narcissism" about the development of ego from the state of "primary narcissism" (which corresponds to closeness to or union with "good feelings" as an object) as follows: *the develop-*

---

*Freud put forward a new theory of anxiety in "Inhibitions, Symptoms and Anxiety". In contrast to the earlier theory ("Freud's first theory of anxiety"), in which the anxiety was seen as the product of transformation of undischarged libido, anxiety was now seen as a signal of threatening danger ("Freud's second theory of anxiety"). We can generalize Freud's revised theory, in which anxiety functioned as a signal, to all affects, and consider all affects to be capable of having a signal function (Joffe & Sandler, "Adaptation, Affects and the Representational World").

ment of object relationships consists in a departure from the close primary relation to the affects of pleasure, well-being, and security and gives rise to a vigorous attempt to recover that relationship. Part of this *"vigorous attempt"* is the obliteration or removal of unpleasant or painful feelings, to the extent that this is possible. The wish to remove whatever is unpleasant, to obliterate it, or to displace it so that it is disowned mobilizes all the resources of the infant, including what we normally refer to as his aggression. (This type of aggression, functioning to gain "good" feelings and to get rid of "bad" ones, should be distinguished from sadistic impulses.[28])

There seems to be a predisposition from birth on for the child to learn to experience the caretaking mother as a source of pleasure and satisfaction, and if all goes well, he very quickly links his subjective experience of his interaction with her with the primary affective pleasurable object. If things do not go well, if the way the child experiences the interaction with the mother is unpleasant, the child may turn to other sources of "good" feeling—perhaps to another person or to an object with whom the child interacts in phantasy. We want to stress that it is not the mother that has become the "good" or "nice" object, but the dynamic gestalt of subjective *experiences* arising from all the interactions between the child and his mother, although the mother will become the representative of this affectively laden gestalt. With the later development of boundaries between self and object the child will attempt to restore his relationship to the earlier pleasurable affective states by making use of the dialogue that has developed between himself and his mother. He will make use of the "mutual cueing" or "perceptual refuelling" described so vividly by Mahler and her colleagues.[29] The refuelling dialogue leads to a relationship with the person as object that can be regarded as essentially a structured role-relationship, a complementary interaction between self and object. This is discussed in detail in Chapter 6, where it is pointed out that, as self–object boundaries develop, the object attains its own identity for the child, who scans the object, interacts with it, and in this way gains psychological nourishment. This is normally associated with reassurance, feelings of security, and a sense of mastery. It is particularly significant, however, that the child's own self is also an object for the child—an object constantly scanned, with whom the child has a continual dialogue.

In the absence of the external object, the relationship can be recreated (after a certain point in development) as a dialogue in the child's conscious or unconscious phantasy life. Just as relationships to others can be regarded as role relationships, so too are relationships, in thought or phantasy, to the various images in the conscious or unconscious wishes and phantasies deriving from the structures we call "internal objects".

To conclude, let us pull some threads together. We can broaden our theoretical base by placing emphasis on the child's wishful impulses and wishful phantasies (and not only on his instinctual drives). We would also maintain:

1. that needs and associated wishes are aroused by disturbances in the basic central (conscious or unconscious) feeling state of the individual; such disturbances are caused not only by drive stimuli and internal conflict, but also by the external world—for example, by the perception of the absence of the object who forms part of a crucial role-relationship, resulting in a lack of "affirmation";

2. that wishes of all sorts contain mental representations of self, of object, and of the interaction between the two; again, the aim of such interactions is to bring about, in a roundabout way, closeness to the primary affective "good" state or object, and distance from (or obliteration of) the primary affective "bad", unpleasant state or object;

3. that the negotiations of early infancy continue into adult life, although we tend to become more inflexible in the roles we demand of others and of ourselves.

To a large extent external object relationships can be conceived of as being wish-fulfilments, sometimes of necessity heavily disguised. So the overt relationship may be considered to be a derivative of an underlying wishful phantasy role-relationship, often radically modified on its path to the surface by some form of defensive activity. Such defensive activity includes all the various forms of projection and externalization. All these processes can be viewed as occurring *intrapsychically*, as part of the internal work of defence and censorship. We also can include in such mental work processes such as projective identification (Klein) and the use of the object as a "container" (Bion), *if we do not conceive of something actually and concretely being put into the other object, but rather think of them as metaphors.*[30] Our view would be that in projective identification it is more that some aspect of the subject's self-representation is defensively placed (or displaced) intrapsychically in phantasy into the subject's mental representation of his object. The underlying internal object relationship and its unconscious phantasy derivative, modified intrapsychically by defensive processes, can then be actualized in a manifest form that may be very different from the deeper unconscious object relationship.* However, the actualization can provide a wish-fulfilment because of the capacity for unconscious "understanding-work" referred to in Chapter 2. This allows an unconscious understanding of the meaning of the manifest relationship, as the fulfilment of a wish, to occur. While childhood relationships may be repeated without much alteration in later life, they may equally be heavily disguised, and it is part of the work of analysis to trace the ways in which this disguise has been created, that is, to examine the defensive distortions of the original unconscious wishes and phantasies embodying a sought-for role-relationship.

The clinical implications of the point of view presented here are extensive. The regulation of conscious and unconscious feelings is placed in the centre of the clinical stage. Interpretation of the feeling state that is closest to the surface becomes a primary consideration in our technical approach, and we include, in our understanding of what may be happening to the patient, the notion that his feeling states may be affected by stimuli that are not necessarily instinctual in origin. We are provided with a view of motivation, conflict, and of various forms of psychopathology and symptoms, in which the control of feelings through the direct or indirect maintenance of specific role relationships is of crucial significance.

---

*A useful distinction can be made between the past unconscious, which is part of the non-experiential realm, and the present unconscious, in what we have called the experiential realm, where percepts, current thoughts, recalled memories, daydreams, feelings—indeed all current subjective experiences— are located. In this framework, internal objects are in the past unconscious, but unconscious wishful phantasies are in the present unconscious.[31]

CHAPTER FIVE

Character traits
and object relations

Introduction

In the past, psychoanalytic theory has held that character traits should be viewed as "discharge" phenomena and compromise formations. Many traits can be better understood, however, as devices for evoking particular types of response in others in order to actualize the wished-for relationships existing in unconscious phantasy. Moreover, some "evocative" character traits create the unconscious illusion of the presence of the love objects.

* * *

As Hermann Nunberg[1] once remarked, "character is an elusive phenomenon." It is now generally accepted that the term is often used synonymously with "personality", referring, as a psychiatric dictionary puts it, to "the characteristic ... behaviour–response patterns that each person evolves, both consciously and unconsciously, as his style of life".[2] The early writers on character and character traits—beginning with Freud, who in 1908 shocked his readers with his paper, "Character and Anal Erotism"[3]—were primarily concerned with understanding particular character traits as surface manifestations of instinctual wishes of one sort or another. This view reflects what can be called a "discharge" theory of character. As Freud expressed it in his paper: "the permanent character-traits are either unchanged prolongations of the original instincts, or sublimations of those instincts, or reaction-formations against them".

The idea that character can reflect defensive compromise was given particular emphasis by the work of Wilhelm Reich,[4] who saw character as arising from infantile instinctual conflict, reflecting in particular the mastery of such conflict by using defences, leading ultimately to the so-called character-armour [*Charakter-panzerung*]. Although Reich did not explicitly consider the way in which adaptation to early social reality contributed to the development of character, this was later remedied by Hartmann, Erikson, Fenichel, and others. An important consequence of Reich's approach was that *character* tended to be equated with *ego*. Thus Fenichel commented that "the dynamic and economic organization of its positive actions and the ways in which the ego combines its various tasks in order to find a satisfactory solution, all of this goes to make up 'character'".[5] Small wonder, then, that Fenichel went on to say that his description of *character* is nearly identical with that previously given for the *ego*.

It should be noted that for Fenichel, as for others before him, character traits differed from neurotic symptoms in that such symptoms were seen as ego-dystonic compromise formations and character traits as ego-syntonic ones—a distinction that, from a present-day perspective, is clearly not entirely valid. It is safe to conclude, however, that with the burgeoning of ego psychology interest in character traits declined. The same has not been true for so-called "character neurosis", or character disorder. The notion of character disturbance has been used, from the beginning, for a whole range of clinical pictures that do not manifest symptoms but "modes of behaviour leading", as Laplanche and Pontalis[6] put it, "to recurrent or permanent difficulty in the patient's relation to his environment". In recent years particular attention has been paid to the narcissistic character disorders, in which the pathology is seen as radically different from that which occurs in the neuroses and in which the patient is usually severely disturbed. Here, too, the idea of character *traits*, as organized units of behaviour or as fixed characteristics or dispositions of the individual, is not given much attention, perhaps because we can now have a fuller view of the structural organization underlying the surface picture.

This chapter is concerned with a particular theme—that of the connection between certain idiosyncrasies or traits of character and the theory of internal object relationships. The general theory of character traits is not discussed, and it should not be thought that the ideas put forward here apply to all traits of character or personality. There is, however, a fruitful area of psychoanalytic investigation still open to us in relation to the function and meaning of certain aspects of character.

The topic can be approached obliquely from the starting-point of a consideration of certain aspects of countertransference. In earlier chapters the view was put forward, in relation to countertransference and role-responsiveness, that concepts such as transference, projection, and externalization could be widened to include the patient's attempts to manipulate or to provoke the analyst into responding in a particular way. It was pointed out that the patient tries, in the transference, to use subtle and for the most part unconscious techniques to impose a way of experiencing and behaving. The patient unconsciously scans his perception of the analyst and adapts to the reactions he perceives. We can assume that the interaction between the two people involved is determined, to a significant degree, by the roles each is trying to impose upon the other—roles that are part of each party's intrapsychic role-relationship at the time. All this relates to the whole spectrum of unconscious needs and wishes, either manifested directly or modified by the individual's defences. What occurs in the analytic relationship, in the transference–countertransference interchange, also occurs outside it, and it seems evident that the dimensions of transference–countertransference are identical with those of object relationships.

Many character traits have the specific function of *actualizing* a particular object-related wishful phantasy by evoking appropriate responses in those around the patient. This is very different from the "discharge" view of a character trait, in which the surface expression is an end-result. It is more a view of certain fixed personality characteristics as "evocative", in the sense that has been described. It is such traits of character that are responsible for "character transferences", which reflect those aspects of the patient's relationship to people (or to special groups of people) that "are not in any way specific to the therapist, but are in the nature of character traits. Such reactions . . . very often are seen in the *earliest* sessions of treatment. Typical of such manifestations is the occurrence in the analysis of a habitual tendency to placate or appease, habitual demandingness, or a sado-masochistic tendency".[7]

An example of a "character transference" would be the case of a child who is frightened of policemen or doctors, or anyone in uniform or authority, who begins treatment by being frightened of the analyst. This might occur, for example, when a patient who habitually externalizes onto adults critical aspects of his superego relates to the analyst in the same way as to any other adult. The distinctive features of this form of relating can be brought out further by considering the example of an adult patient who appears late for an analytic session. This may be the consequence of a specific transference situation arising in treatment, in which, for example, an anxiety about a homosexual attachment to the analyst has been activated. On the other hand, the lateness might reflect a characteristic tendency in the patient to be late.

It is possible to speculate on whether the analyst's responses (including countertransference responses in the broad sense of the term) to "character transference" from the side of the patient are different in quality from the range of his normal countertransference responses to transference proper. It seems likely that there are important differences that might merit closer study.

Perhaps the most striking constellations of character traits that frequently show themselves in "character transference" are those that relate to sado-masochistic tendencies within the individual. Every analyst knows of the provocative and evocative capacities of patients with such tendencies, which have been caricatured in various ways. Patients with sado-masochistic character tendencies are often adept at enticing the analyst (and others in the extra-analytic world) to react critically in a way that immediately evokes the most damning criticism and condemnation of the analyst by the patient. Such sado-masochistic character tendencies are more than a simple tendency to express a wish or constellation of wishes coming from the depths to the surface as a consequence of the analytic work. What we see is a mechanism that *entices* others to give a particular sort of response, a response that must be wish-fulfilling in the sense that all object relationships involve wishes, not only for instinctual gratification, but also for particular sorts of affirmation. The sado-masochistic patient needs the sado-masochistic dialogue, not only to gratify his sadistic and masochistic wishes, but also to secure the good feelings and safety that accompany the actualization of a wishful phantasy based on an internalized childhood relationship.

The view has been taken that the particular content of the selfobject dialogue is heavily influenced by the child's earliest experiences in interaction with his objects, influenced both from the side of the child and from that of the object. It is abundantly clear that the idiosyncrasies of the interchange between child and parent, even in the earliest period of life, remain as part of the object relationship. Moreover, the child learns to initiate wish-fulfilling responses from the object by using various mechanisms and signals that are involved in the dialogue. It should be stressed that even painful and distressing relationships can be safety-giving, reassuring, and affirming for many different reasons, as well as being instinctually satisfying, and the so-called sado-masochistic type of relationship exemplifies this extremely well. Many techniques used by the child in the dialogue with his objects can be regarded as object-related character traits, or as the precursors of these, which are neither instinctual derivatives nor defences against them, nor even combinations of the two, *but, rather, devices elaborated to evoke specific wished-for responses in others.*

The responses of others evoked by character traits enable the wished-for and valued dialogues or role relationships that constitute internal object relationships to be realized or actualized by prompting real external objects to respond in particular ways. This occurs in ordinary life and in the psychoanalytic situation in the transference, whether this be considered to be character transference, so-called transference manifestations, or transference neurosis. Within this framework we can see how character traits can have an essential function in the present in helping to achieve (or attempting to achieve) the wish-fulfilment inherent in object relationships. However, everything that has been discussed so far is in the realm of interpersonal relationships—of "transactions" between people—and in order for our argument to be truly psychoanalytic, we need to expand it further. This is perhaps best done by reference to an example.

An analytic patient, Mr P., was described in Chapter 4. It may be useful to give the account of some aspects of his analysis in greater detail. His analyst reported as follows, with regard to the patient's habitual tendency to procrastinate.

> Mr P. would delay writing his reports, or preparing papers for presentation, although he usually managed to succeed in getting them done at the last moment. He told me, "I can't 'produce' until I feel that a catastrophe might happen. It is as if I have to wait until just before some awful explosion might occur, and then I can usually force myself to sit down and work." In a previous analysis this tendency had been linked with the gaining of erotic pleasure through anal retentiveness, as witnessed by his childhood constipation, and with the satisfaction that he obtained through his sadistic control of his own faeces. It had also been connected with his phantasies of being able to control his world in an omnipotent fashion.
>
> As his analysis proceeded, he described many problems connected with his delaying and holding back, and there is no doubt that this character trait had a distinctly "anal" quality, as classically described. However, after about a year of analysis he realized that he had kept postponing paying my account for some weeks, always finding one reason or another to delay payment. At the beginning of the session, when he had confessed that he had again postponed writing a cheque, he told me that he was sure that I was extremely angry with him. He told me that I had looked angry when he saw me, and that he was sure now that I would explode with rage if he went on postponing it any longer. He added that I must be so full of rage that I could surely think of nothing else. (I was, indeed, mildly irritated by his delay in paying, and—as reported in Chapter 4—had at times felt frustrated by the patient's inability to come to the point in an account of what had happened the previous day.) I was now able to show him that he had

used delaying payment as a way of trying to create a situation in which he felt that I was on the point of exploding, while having all my attention focused on him. There was ample evidence that this repeated a situation that had occurred frequently in his childhood, in which he would not do things that his mother had asked him to do, and she would respond to his provocation by nagging him, getting angrier and angrier. While she nagged him, he told me, she would turn her attention away from the other children and from her husband. He had learned to recognize just how far he could go and would finally do what she had wanted just before she "exploded". I should mention that this patient had a brother, some two and a half years his junior, who, as a sickly child from birth, had "stolen"—as the patient put it—his mother's attention from the moment of his birth. He went on to tell me that at times when he found it difficult to work, he could "almost hear the voice of his mother nagging at him".

It is possible to see that the tendency to delay had, in this patient, a dimension additional to those usually described for this typically "anal" character trait—that of the specific object relationship involved. A major function of this patient's delaying was to create the equivalent of "being nagged by mother". However, although it was possible to see the operation of this mechanism as it developed in the transference, this patient was not normally a provoker of others to be angry with him, or even to "nag" at him (although, in the heat of the transference, he managed to provoke irritation in the analyst). For the most part, he managed to deal with his colleagues in an adequate way, and his dialogue with his mother—or, rather, with her current representative—occurred generally in his unconscious phantasy life, although he had to enact his *delaying* in order to re-experience *in phantasy* the relationship with his mother in which she attended to him by nagging.

The "transaction" of this patient with his mother was more of an intrapsychic transaction than those considered earlier; his dialogue with his mother, which was reassuring and gratifying to him and which took place in phantasy rather than in reality, emerged in the transference as something more than a simple "character transference".

If we assume that his character trait involved the provoking of an object and was useless without the appropriate response from the object—that is, that it was a method of attaining a wish-fulfilling actualization—then we have to ask how this is possible with an object *in phantasy*, without a significant amount of role evocation in reality. We would have no difficulty in answering this if we were dealing with a psychotic patient who hallucinated the mother and her nagging. One could simply say that the patient actualized the wished-for interaction with the object by a hallucinatory perception of the object, just as occurs in the dream; one could then speak of the various disguises and transformations that occur in the hallucination as the hallucination-work, just as one speaks of the dream-work. It can be assumed that the maternal introject consists of a structural organization, based upon the experiences in childhood of interaction with the mother and distorted by a great variety of the patient's projections and externalizations during his development. The relationship to this introject, in its derivative form in unconscious phantasy, would be the basis for the nagging-and-being-nagged dialogue with the mother, which would occur in the hallucinatory experience of the hypothetical psychotic patient of whom we are speaking. Yet Mr P. did not hallucinate—he was largely unaware of what was happening. The apparent paradox can be dealt with by introducing the concept of *subliminal, unconscious,* or *preconscious* illusion—in the sense of a particular subjective experience not based on the current perception of external reality, but arising as if it were so based. This is a difficult idea to formulate and probably an implausible one at first sight, because it seems to involve a contradiction. How can we have an illusion that something or someone is present and not see them? And yet, on reflection, the idea is not implausible. It is now well established that we can perceive below the threshold of conscious perception, that information can reach us subliminally and affect us profoundly. It would be quite appropriate to describe the phenomenon as a preconscious illusion. The assertion here is that we can, and often do, create such illusions in our preconscious phantasy life in order to actualize our unconscious wishes, and that illusions of this sort are normally kept below the threshold of normal perception. They hover just beneath it, so to speak, but the capacity for reality testing makes all the difference here between normality and psychosis. The relation between (descriptively) unconscious phantasies and reality is delicately traced by Arlow[8] in two papers relating phantasy to disturbances of conscious experience, as well as to memory and reality testing.

Mr P. habitually procrastinated, using a specific technique (or, we could say, a character trait) that he had developed as part of the object-relationship dialogue with his mother, as a way of recreating her presence below the threshold of conscious awareness; but he established more than her unconscious presence. He recreated an unconscious dialogue with her that was a central part of his wished-for interaction with her. By experiencing her nagging, albeit below the threshold of conscious awareness, he could feel that he could obtain her exclusive attention. He could gain a sort of reassurance and affirmation, as well as satisfying libidinal and rivalrous wishes. His habitual postponing, although it may have had its roots in the anal phase of development, was a technique for evoking the subliminal, intrapsychically real experience of the transaction with mother.

The notion of mental "presences" is, of course, not new. In the 1930s, Edoardo Weiss[9] described a phenomenon that he called "psychic presence". We can extend this to the concept of unconscious psychic presence and relate the existences of presences with whom we interact to the derivatives in unconscious phantasy of the structures regarded as internal objects.

It should be clear by now that a useful way to approach the study of character traits is by asking first what the function of the character trait is, and next, how it operates to fulfil that function. It can then be seen how such traits are not only the expression of instinctual wishes, the product of defences against such wishes, or combinations of the two, but also ways of evoking responses from our significant objects or their present-day representatives. These latter are representations of actual persons in the real world or represented in unconscious phantasy—part of an illusory world that is unconsciously created and unconsciously perceived. They may be part of transactions with people who actually exist outside ourselves, or unconscious transactions with phantasied objects. Such transactions are not, of course, simple repetitions of early relationship dialogues, as they are affected by the displacements and modifications that result from the operation of our defences;

and such object-related dialogues, although always wish-fulfilling, may be as much defensive as instinctually gratifying. Above all, they function to provide safety, affirmation, and well-being.

This discussion has intentionally been limited to some aspects of character, but the arguments put forward here can be developed in several different directions. What is true for so-called character traits may also be true for many symptoms, or for a variety of aspects of behaviour. The role of character development in relation to techniques for obtaining narcissistic supplies is another important area for exploration. All analysts are familiar with the difference between the narcissistic patient who needs the role-response of admiration and the patient who satisfies his narcissism in his phantasy life alone. Perhaps, above all, what these considerations may lead us toward is the detailed study of both overt and covert aspects of personality and character in terms of their relation to the dialogues that form and subsequently arise from our object relations. Man is a social animal, but as psychoanalysts we must know that man lives simultaneously in two societies—one we know as the people in the real external world, and the other in a phantom world of unconscious phantasy in which the objects are created, updated, recreated, and subjectively experienced in relation to the self. We interact with our objects in both these worlds and spend much of our waking life trying to modify ourselves and our environments so that the discrepancy between the two is minimized. From these attempts flow transference, projection, rationalization, and many other familiar everyday phenomena.

CHAPTER SIX

Stranger anxiety
and internal objects

Introduction

T he point of departure for the ideas in this chapter is the concept of stranger anxiety (or eight-month anxiety) observed and written about by René Spitz, with whose name the concept is indissolubly linked.[1] Following this, there is a detailed examination of the function of the self–object dialogue, as well as the role of the dialogue one has with one's own self in providing affective sustenance—in particular, feelings of reassurance and security. What follows is based on a Spitz Memorial Lecture.

* * *

Following a discussion of some aspects of the phenomenon of stranger anxiety, I present clinical material from an adult psychoanalytic case to demonstrate a striking correspondence between an adult mode of functioning and the "stranger anxiety" of the infant. Perhaps of special interest are the technical implications of viewing a particular type of anxiety in an adult patient as paralleling stranger anxiety.

In his developmental theory Spitz lays much emphasis on what he has called "the dialogue"[2]—the interaction and mutual responsiveness to cues—which occurs between the infant and his mother. The child's initial behaviour is seen as based on its biological needs and reactions, to which the mother responds in a way that must leave its mark on the infant. By the age of three months or before, the child shows the well-known smiling response.[3] According to Spitz this is a sign of the recognition of the familiar, and the baby's responsive smile becomes a crucial part of his side of his dialogue with the people around him. All the evidence points to mutual cueing occurring extremely early.[4] At its very beginning, the response is not specific to any given person but may be given to a certain perceptual configuration, a gestalt consisting of two eyes, a forehead, a nose, and movement.[5] It has an anticipatory character, represents part of an exchange of signals, and testifies to the child's ongoing psychological dialogue with his surroundings. We know, however, that it is likely that at this stage the psychological boundaries between the baby and his surroundings are fluid and ill-defined, and so the smiling response probably starts as a reflex, based upon innate "givens", and is increasingly linked with the recognition of the familiar.

During the following months, significant and rapid psychological development takes place. The child's responses within the mother–child dialogue become much more specific, and he is more sharply attuned to changes in his subjective experience. In the first months a very specific mode of dialogue will normally have developed between the child and his mother—unique for this particular mother–child couple and involving a whole history of mutual cues and adaptations by both child and mother. The concept of mother–infant *synchrony* is relevant here.[6] By now the child's capacity to scan and to search its environment for information has developed to a significant extent. Thus the infant usually reacts by smiling and often with other signs of pleasure to the approach of any person; but by about eight months of age, sometimes earlier or relatively suddenly, he will show displeasure when an unfamiliar person approaches. This so-called stranger anxiety will range from a mild reaction (e.g. a slowing down of activity) to severe panic. There may be simply a "bashful" averting of the eyes, a burying of the face in the blankets, or even fits of screaming or weeping.

For Spitz, this is "a turning-point in the unfolding of object relations, a progression from the precursor of the object to the establishment of the object proper".[7] Spitz postulates that at approximately eight months the child becomes capable of attachment to a *specific* person and consequently becomes vulnerable to the anxiety about losing that object—the mother or her substitute (nowadays we would date this much earlier). Spitz's thesis was that the face of the stranger now evokes in the child an expectation that we, as adults, can verbalize as "Mummy is coming". The stranger's unfamiliar face and movements demolish this expectation, and, according to Spitz, the infant discovers that, as *we* would say, "Mummy is gone—this is not Mummy".[8] In the classic description of stranger anxiety, as given by Spitz, the baby will immediately turn away from the face of the stranger, unable to bear the anxiety of the loss of the mother. Broadly speaking, Spitz equates stranger anxiety with the most primitive form of separation anxiety.[9] I think that Spitz has, in this formulation, condensed and oversimplified a complicated sequence of processes, and that it is appropriate to reconsider the relation of stranger anxiety to the fear of the loss of the object. My justification for going into this is that I believe the point to be of clinical as well as theoretical significance. John Benjamin[10] has shown that, before the appearance of stranger anxiety, the infant who does not yet have a fear of strangers may still react with fear of "the strange". This includes such things as loud noises, people behaving differently from what the infant is used to, or indeed any grossly unusual sensory experience. Nevertheless, if the strange experience is not sudden, many children can feel sufficiently secure that they will react with curiosity and inquisitiveness. The appearance of the stranger does not yet produce an intense disruption of the child's subjective feelings of well-being.

During this time the child is experimenting, as it were, with the progressively forming boundaries between himself and his mother. The object is becoming "created" out of the subjective mother–child matrix, as is the child's self-representation as distinct from that of the object. By about seven or eight months of age he has reached a critical period in his psychological reaction to his mother, necessarily forced on him by the development of his self–object boundaries. Other persons, including the mother, have thus far been to a significant extent a part of his own self, but the to-and-fro of his psychological development leads him to a greater degree of awareness of separateness, and thus of the specific characteristics of the mother, the most important other person in his life. The ongoing and developing dialogue with the mother suddenly becomes much more important for him as a source of comfort, security, and well-being, as a means of counteracting his growing awareness of her as a person separate from himself, and the resultant diminution in what has been called his "infantile omnipotence". He becomes much more aware than before of the mother's specific features and characteristics. Parallel with this, he becomes increasingly conscious of specific characteristics of his own self and of his own specific responses to his mother. His perception of both himself and his mother becomes more acute and differentiated, and he has to be able to carry on the dialogue with his mother across the growing barrier of separateness.

Now, when confronted with a stranger, he may react with a moment of utter disorganization, panic, and distress, because the expectation of perceiving the familiar "mother-who-is-distinct-from-but-was-part-of-me" is suddenly disrupted by perceptual information that does not "fit". It is unfamiliar, unsafe, and "strange" and intrudes into the familiar perceptual-motor dialogue with mother, a dialogue that normally enables him to bridge the gap of separateness and to restore the earlier good feelings associated with the original close union when mother and self were indistinguishable. At this point his own ego development and his increased perceptiveness and capacity for differentiation render him extremely vulnerable.

If one were to try to put the child's feelings into words, one might say that the experience of sensory disruption by the appearance of the unexpected and unwanted stranger is the feeling: "This person does not belong to the world of my mother and me, and intrudes nastily into it". We could say that the child's subjective experience is one of perceptual *dissonance* (to borrow a term from Festinger[11]) that, in its most extreme form, can be regarded as an experience of overwhelming panic. This, in my view, would then be *followed* by a turning to the familiar, in an attempt to replace dissonance by consonance, to gain the security of the experience of the dialogue with what is known and recognized—above all, to be as close as possible to mother. In a sense, we could regard this "turning to the familiar" as defensive or adaptive. In mild cases, simply looking for mother and then keeping her in sight may be enough, but, inevitably, from this point there is a heightened fear of the loss of the experience of what is familiar, predictable, satisfying, and comforting—a fear that shows itself on the surface as the specific fear of loss of the mother. This is a primitive reaction, essentially linked with the child's fear of loss of the heavily invested reciprocal dialogue between himself and the mother. Fear of loss of the object is different from a fear of the strange, although the two may very rapidly become linked, in that the intrusion of the strange may almost immediately evoke the fear of loss of the familiar, in particular of the perception of the familiar object and the reassuring interaction with it. Although fear of strangers is placed by Spitz at the age of eight months, the potential for its occurrence and the associated fear of object loss continues after its first appearance. It is worth saying that there is as yet no conclusive evidence that the child who shows intense stranger anxiety in the second half of the first year will have similarly intense reactions to strangers in later life.

At this point I want to make a few comments on what I have called *dissonance*, although I do not want to go into its relation to anxiety here. One source of experiential dissonance is the failure of the child's expectations to be met by its actual new subjective experience. We can consider such dissonance, if it remains within tolerable limits, as one of the normal motivating forces in the progressive development of the psychic apparatus throughout life. If it is not catastrophic, it functions as a spur to intrapsychic adaptation, of which progressive structural differentiation is the essence. For progressive adaptation, however, the dissonance needs to be "held" by the child's other sources of safety and well-being, and by his capacity to explore possible new solutions and ways of coping. Dissonance beyond a certain degree is extremely unpleasant, but its mastery and its replacement by perceptual and cognitive *consonance*, when expectations are met by experience, is pleasant, reassuring, and even exciting.

I cannot resist the temptation to draw a parallel between the stranger panic, which arises because the tenuous psychological schema or structure of "mother-as-separate-from-me" cannot encompass the dissonant experience of the stranger's face, on the one hand, and the *catastrophic reactions* shown by certain patients with organic structural brain damage, on the other. Consider Kurt Goldstein's description, given many years ago, of organic catastrophic reactions, bearing in mind the infant's panic reaction to the stranger. He comments:

> Now let us observe one of our patients. Here is a man with a lesion of the frontal lobe, to whom we present a problem in simple arithmetic. He is unable to solve it. Just looking at him, we can see a great deal more than his arithmetical failure. He looks dazed, changes colour, becomes agitated, anxious. . . . He is now sullen, evasive, exhibits temper. . . . It takes some time before it is possible to continue the examination. Because the patient is so disturbed in his whole behaviour, we call situations of this kind *catastrophic situations*.[12]

Goldstein goes on to point out that the organism needs to maintain constancy, and its preservation and tranquillity "requires a determinate environment or a certain kind of milieu". He adds that forceful environmental events

> produce not orderly harmonious responses, but rather disorderly, disharmonious, defective performances, climaxing in catastrophic situations with all their concomitants, particularly anxiety. . . . Upsetting stimuli may arise in any situation, and then coming, so to speak, out of the blue, they fall upon the patient with the redoubled force of the unexpected. . . . We observe again and again that patients will start violently upon being suddenly addressed. Nor is it even necessary that what is said to them should contain anything irritating. What acts upon them as an irritant is the mere fact that the stimulus comes from a situation not belonging to their present milieu.

This description of the effect of damage to organic structures also applies, in my view, to the fragile psychological structures that the child is building up at about eight months of age. His stranger anxiety (or stranger panic) reflects a normal developmental fragility at a critical period when self- and object-representations are beginning to be differentiated but are not yet well established.

We find the same sort of catastrophic panic in certain border-line and psychotic cases, as well as in congenitally blind children, whom we have had the special opportunity to observe at the Anna Freud Centre. It seems clear that normal stranger anxiety is only a special case of a more general phenomenon, one that has to do with the inability of the individual to "contain", within the structures he has at his disposal, the intrusion of the markedly unfamiliar. The unfamiliar creates dissonance and directly reduces feelings of security,[13] and, as an immediate consequence, the person turns to the safe and familiar. Here again one cannot fail to be struck by Goldstein's description of a brain-damaged adult:

> The activities that engross the patient need not have any great value in themselves; their usefulness to him consists in their protective character. This behaviour reveals that the patient is utterly incapable of the contemplative attitude of the healthy man, cannot take himself for granted, or play the part of a detached spectator.[14]

For those who fear that I may by now have strayed too far from psychoanalysis, let me say at once that I am fully aware that I have concentrated my discussion on the way an external situation can produce a change in the child. However, wishes arising from within the child may equally create experiences of dissonance, even at a very early age. Later, unconscious primitive strivings and the wishes, phantasies, and fears associated with them may be extremely dissonant in that they are felt to be intrusive and disruptive, the instigators of conflict, and have to be defended against or dealt with by whatever means are available. The motives for defence here include the need to avoid the experience of disruptive dissonance and to regain the pleasurable and harmonious feelings of well-being and security.

I should like to take up a point from which I digressed earlier. The awareness of separateness, of the child's boundary between himself and his mother, renders him threatened and vulnerable. I suggested that, making use of Spitz's idea, we can conceive of the child attempting to maintain the secure feelings associated with the earlier state of perceptual "oneness" with the mother by continuing his perceptual interaction with her in the form of a *dialogue* with her—a dialogue that can bridge the separateness experienced by the child. In this context the observations on young infants reported by Margaret Mahler and her colleagues have the greatest significance.[15] To quote:

> From about 7 to 8 months of age we have found the visual pattern of "checking back to mother" ... to be the most important fairly regular sign of beginning ... differentiation. In fact it appears to be the most important normal pattern of cognitive and emotional development. The baby begins comparative scanning. ... He becomes interested in "mother" and seems to compare her with "other", the unfamiliar with the familiar, feature by feature. He seems to familiarize himself more thoroughly, as it were, with what is mother, what feels, tastes, smells, looks like, and has the "clang" of mother. ... He starts to discriminate between mother and he or she or it that looks, feels, moves differently from, or similarly to, mother.

Mahler and her co-workers go on to describe how the "checking back to mother" relates to what they call the mutual "cueing" between mother and child. Mahler's use of the idea of "refuelling" refers to the way in which the young child constantly *returns* to supply itself with feelings of security and well-being through visual and other contact with the mother. This recurs and represents both the child's emotional tie to the mother and a source of protection in terms of the child's need to deal with the threats posed by his separateness from the mother. We all know how the young child, however interested he may be in other things, constantly "checks back" to mother. We could say that he repeatedly turns to her for "affirmation". If, for some reason, he notices that mother is missing, he often experiences extreme distress. At this point I should like to combine two terms introduced by Mahler and Spitz and to say that the child needs the *refuelling dialogue* with the mother, to allow himself to feel safe in being relatively independent of her. Inner sources of security are not yet enough—the consonance of the repeated perception that mother is there, providing affirmation, is vitally necessary. It is, of course, not only the toddler's growing confidence in his capacity to "master" his world that is insufficient at this stage. His developing capacity for thought, play, and phantasy cannot provide him as yet with the basic reassurance that he gains from the perceptual contact with and recognition of the mothering person. Perceptual contact includes the child's experiences gained through all his sensory modalities, and the experience of physical contact (as in cuddling and hugging) is crucially important.

With the growth of self–object boundaries and the associated experience of separateness, the object gradually develops an identity of its own in the mind of the child, and it is the repeated scanning of that constant so-called "libidinal" object, who interacts with the child, even at a distance, which provides a refuelling, a nutriment, a nourishment for the child's sense of security and feeling of mastery, that helps to guard the child against experiencing catastrophic panic in the face of the unfamiliar.

However, with self–object differentiation, another constant object, one with an equally enduring identity, also emerges for the child. *This is the child's own self.* Here I am using the term "self" in the same way as I might otherwise refer to "object"—that is, as a mental representation that has both structural and experiential aspects, just as the object has, in the mind of the child. It develops a continuity in time, becomes stable and constant, and, like the object-representation, develops an enduring identity. This conceptual parallel between self and object allows us, I believe, to get closer to solving the problem of creating a useful definition of the self and of identity.

We are very aware of the infant's dialogue with his real object (which may, of course, be continued into later life and subsequently added to by dialogue with objects in conscious and unconscious phantasy and thought). However, the scanning of "phantasied" or "imagined" object images does not provide any significant degree of refuelling until the child is significantly older. Until then, the child is essentially dependent on the perception of the external object for refuelling and consequent feelings of security. In addition, the child's scanning of the object and the process of refuelling is obvious to the observer. As Spitz would say, we have clear external "indicators". I should like to postulate that we have a parallel process occurring, not so evident from the outside, in which the child *constantly and automatically also scans and has a dialogue with his own self to get refuelling and affirmation, through the perception of cues, that his self is his old familiar self, that it is no stranger to him.* He is normally constantly gaining a feeling of consonance from his own self-representation. If, on the other hand, he perceives a sudden change in his own self-image, he may be exposed to dissonance or even stranger panic in the same way as when confronted with a strange person when he expects to see the object. Thus the source of dissonance may be external or internal. The child may then attempt to protect himself from danger by increased refuelling through action in which he alters himself, which makes his self-representation more affirming, more reassuring. Such action and alteration of the self-representation in the face of dissonance or panic may take various forms. The child may, for example, keep absolutely still, systematically "taking stock" of himself. He may rush to be cuddled and held by mother, or he may turn to playing with a familiar toy or in a familiar corner of the room. In this way he recreates a state of security based on the re-experiencing of specific past consonant dialogues. He may also make use of primitive defences and adaptive mechanisms (such as rudimentary identification) to modify his self-perception as well as his perception of the external world. In the early years, of course, scanning of the self goes hand-in-hand with scanning of the object, and as long as the child is dependent on his perception of the object for feelings of safety, the refuelling from the object will play a greater part in providing feelings of safety than scanning of the self alone. However, there is a normal recurring and reassuring dialogue with the self, just as there is a constant perceptual dialogue with the object.

The processes I have been discussing are normally subsumed under much broader headings, such as "separation anxiety", "fear of loss of love", and "fear of loss of the object". While the processes I have described are essentially normal, they can move into the realm of the pathological, into the areas of disturbances of narcissism, of pathogenic projections and externalizations, and of severe inhibitions. We may see the development of pathology based on the construction of a "false self"[16] or an "as if" character.[17] In these there are great changes in the self-representation and in the dialogue with objects, in which the child may grossly distort his attitudes and behaviour (and thus create a new self-representation that he can scan) in order to avoid the dissonance and panic that accompanies "simply being himself" (that is, possessing an "unacceptable" self-representation). By creating varieties of false self, he attempts to create and maintain a reciprocal and comforting dialogue with himself and with the object. In clinging to his dialogue with a false self, he can feel secure. In this way he disowns a more natural and spontaneous aspect of himself in relation to the object. He may, it should be added, equally create a "false object", either by forcing the object into a particular role or, more commonly, by distorting his perception of the object (by altering the object-representation) to make it safe and reassuring. Idealization of the object is a common way of doing this, but other mechanisms may be employed (e.g. the "splitting of ambivalence" so that only loving feelings are felt towards the object and felt to come from the object).

In the account of the case that follows, I attempt to illustrate some of the processes described in the previous paragraph. The case can be regarded as one in which the disturbance is not primarily the outcome of neurotic conflict; rather, it can be considered as one illustrating some clinical consequences in an adult of a deviant development, based on a defect existing from early childhood. It is my belief that something went wrong in the "refuelling dialogue" with object and self early in this patient's life. She made use of a particular (and pathogenic) mode of adaptation, which enabled her to cope with and to integrate the strange with the familiar in a particular way that later led her into difficulties. The persisting developmental defect, it seemed, coloured her reactions within each phase of development.

> My patient, Mrs B., came for what she regarded as "counselling" because her husband had entered analysis to get help for his sexual problems. The patient was 39 years old and looked much younger than her age. She had the body of an adolescent, with short blonde hair and large blue eyes. Her movements were somewhat affected, at times theatrical, and hardly ever spontaneous. She wore clothes that were quite inappropriate for her age, and I learned later that she often borrowed clothing from her daughter, aged 13. In the initial interview she spoke of her husband in a matter-of-fact way, and of her two children, aged 8 and 13. Mrs B. told me that she was studying to become a school psychologist, that she was married to a very successful engineer, that the marriage had deteriorated and the relationship with her husband was very strained. For about a year they

had no proper sexual relationship, as her husband suffered from premature ejaculation. She said that she was the fourth and youngest child, with twin sisters five years older than herself and a brother eight years older. Her mother was still alive but had remarried after being divorced. Her father had died when she was at college. Mrs B. indicated that her family was a wealthy one. Her maternal grandmother, who had survived her own husband's early death, was described as having been like a royal personage around whom the whole family gathered in awed respect and admiration. The maternal grandmother was socially very ambitious and ruled her family with an iron fist.

I took Mrs B. on as a patient not because I was fully convinced that she was suitable for once-weekly psychotherapy, but primarily because her husband's analyst convinced me that she was in need of help. I thought that I could provide some support for her while her husband was in analysis. From the beginning, although she often acknowledged intellectually that she must in some way contribute to the marital tension and told me that she had read that sexual problems involve both partners, it quickly became clear that she could not tolerate the idea that she could in any way be to blame for the difficulties. She denied, externalized, and disavowed any responsibility in her marital problems. Moreover, she had a constant need to see herself as a "helping" person whose deep concern and care for people made her very special. This self-image clearly provided her with much comfort and "affirmation".

As the weeks passed and she told me not only of her relationship with her husband but also of her relationships with her children and her friends, I became increasingly amazed at the degree of her underlying anxiety, which she denied completely. Her talking in the session consisted in presenting a series of disconnected points, and she would rush from one topic to another, seemingly convinced that I had completely followed her train of reasoning. When I asked a question or attempted to clarify an obscurity in what she had told me she would dash into further disconnected communications, often looking very frightened. By this time I had the impression that she regularly experienced even the most simple question as intrusive, threat-ening, and attacking.

I tried to take up her material in the transference in terms of the repetition of childhood fears. I attempted, for example, to com-pare the therapeutic situation with an examination, and sug-gested that she felt anxious at the thought that I might criticize her, that she felt exposed and in danger of being humiliated and ridiculed. At first she did not appear to be able to take what I said any further than its immediate *concrete* context and would assure me that she knew very well from my facial expression that I was not laughing at her. Very gradually, I tried to inter-pret that, although she knew it was not an examination situa-tion, nevertheless part of her might feel threatened by the interview, just as I guessed inside herself she often felt criti-cized and afraid. Usually she seemed able to accept this for a brief moment, but she would soon push my comments aside, either telling me how absurd, infantile and ridiculous such anxieties were or assuring me that she had lately made great progress in overcoming her panicky states. In the here-and-now of the sessions she assured me that she felt no anxiety at all, only intense pleasure at being in therapy. It was striking that in Mrs B.'s reactions to my comments there was a kind of reflex-like panic that forced her to deny any internal emotional stress and to cling automatically to some concrete island of security, based on denial and negation and the preservation of me as the "perfect" object.

The more her anxiety and distress increased, the more she had to idealize me. The sessions were, she assured me, the high-lights of her existence. She often concluded her sessions by telling me that she was filled with new understanding and insight, that her admiration for my skill and knowledge was boundless. However, the more she idealized me, the more des-perate I felt, because I experienced being quite helpless, unable to make real sense of the disorganized bits of information she brought to me. I could not decide whether she was a neurotic with severe anxieties, a so-called "borderline" case, someone with a profound character disorder, or even prepsychotic. I should say that although she had many anal–sadistic elements in her personality, she did not seem to me to be attempting to create, as so many patients do, a sado-masochistic relationship in the transference. It was more that she evoked in me, in addition to a feeling of confusion, a sense of her desperation and her frightening internal isolation. Later I was able to understand something of my countertransference reaction.

After a few months she asked whether she could come into analysis, giving as her reason that she had learned so much from the once weekly sessions that analysis would teach her even more. After some thought I agreed to this, in the hope that seeing her five times a week, with the use of the couch, would enable me to understand what was going on. Upon her entering daily treatment, several things emerged. She reacted to lying down with an even greater degree of compulsive and disjointed talking. I had the impression that she was racing from one topic to another, talking to me rather than associating, all of this being clearly accompanied by feelings of panic. Simultaneously, her idealization of me increased, and she was forever reassuring me about how much insight she had acquired and how her behaviour had improved since the beginning of her analysis. She also often told me of situations in which she had been "wonderful" in the handling of some crisis or other at home, in her behaviour with friends, or in the way she looked when she had gone to a party. Whenever possible, I tried to take up the fact that she seemed extremely anxious about what I would think of her and that she appeared to be making gigantic efforts to feel praised and admired by me, just as in her daily life she tried desperately to be praised by her family and friends and to feel praised "inside herself". I also verbalized that, by not praising her, I was a great source of frustration and anxiety for her, in that I was not being the perfect, loving, praising object that would reassure her.

During this period of treatment, it became evident that, outside the analysis, she was massively identified with her (idealized) picture of me, seeing herself as someone who was essentially playing a psychotherapeutic role with her "patients", colleagues, husband, and children. When she told me with pride of the advice she gave, the omnipotent and controlling aspects of her behaviour towards others became clear. Sometimes the inappropriateness of what she would tell others and would do to them and the apparent self-satisfaction with which this was done quite horrified me, and I was often tempted to understand this material as representing an attempt to provoke me into some sort of verbal attack on her. What made me hesitate to interpret this was my increasing awareness that what she did was driven by a blind panic that prevented her from listening to others before rushing in with advice. This completely paralleled what was happening in the analysis, where she was continually compelled to interrupt me practically before I had opened my mouth, rushing to anticipate what I would say. She continually berated herself for what she expected me to accuse her of, would assure me that she was changing, or announce that she had, through my help, gained tremendous insight.

An example of this is shown by the following: during a session she presented her material in a way that was relatively coherent for her. She talked at length of her husband's coolness and aloofness, of how his reading the paper at breakfast drove her insane, of how he did not even look at her when she spoke, so that she did not know how he felt about her or whether he was ever aware of her presence. She also told me of many friends who had complimented her on a variety of achievements, and how she had told her children that they were really very lucky to have a mother who understood them so well. During this session she had spoken of her daughter, who had greatly admired an evening dress the patient had worn for a dinner party the night before. Her husband, on the contrary, had only commented that she looked "skinny". This had made her furious, tears of anger coming to her eyes, and she had angrily told him that her friends had said to her that she was a most attractive woman. At that point we had reached the end of the session, and I commented on how painful it must be for her to have to lie down and not be able to see my face, because she wanted so much to have a visible response from me so as to be reassured.

The next day she told me what a "tremendous" learning experience my remark had provided for her. She commented that she had been able to look at the faces of her clients (schoolchildren and their parents) with an expression of great sympathy and warmth, and that this had been of tremendous value to her all day. It made her feel a better, more effective professional worker.

Gradually I came to understand that when she spoke of her insights, the notion of psychological understanding and of a psychologically irrational inner life had no meaning for her. Of paramount importance for her was the way she behaved, the impression she would give, and what she believed others might think of her, so that she could maintain a reassuring flow of "good" feelings about herself. Everything that was unconscious—that is, unknown to her—was strange and alien, and as a consequence was terrifying and had to be rejected and denied. What she had to reject was awareness of any angry and uncontrollable phantasied dialogue between herself and representations of her internal objects. Here we can see her desperate need to maintain a "false self" as well as a "false object" that she could scan, check back to, that could give her "affirmation" and provide her with a "refuelling dialogue".

This patient's intense difficulty in communicating a description of any experience in the here-and-now involving her feelings was striking. Even an incident of the previous day, if she had been emotionally involved, would be presented in disconnected fragments. The most coherent account that she could bring would be her intellectually worked-over interpretation of what had happened, rather than a report of the occurrence. She could never tell me in a straightforward way what had happened, presenting instead her intellectual and theoretical after-constructions.

During the first year of analysis she brought very few dreams, and even these could not be given directly but came complete with interpretations, and for a long while it was impossible to separate one from the other. As our work proceeded, the main line of development was in her capacity to see that when she told me of how much her friends praised or admired her, or how stupid, angry, or jealous her children or her colleagues were, she was really describing ideas and feelings she had about herself, which she projected indiscriminately onto others. She would also use and manipulate her friends so that they would tell her how excellent she was. There were endless variations on this theme. For example, she told me that she had organized a special speed-reading class for her younger child, who had great difficulty in coping with his reading assignments at school. When she visited his school on open day, the form teacher told her that her son was the best reader in the class and congratulated her. She was quite triumphant when she reported this. However, what I learned later threw a different light on this episode. The teacher had been most surprised to hear that her son had attended special reading classes because he had always been among the very best readers in the class. It was Mrs B. who had severe difficulties in her childhood in learning to read and spell, and later in concentrating when reading and learning. She had attended many remedial classes, which had been a source of deep humiliation and had not helped her much. It seemed that the very fact that she needed remedial teaching filled her with feelings of shame. At the beginning of her analysis she read very little, and this was a source of embarrassment to her within her very intellectual family. She could not bear the slowness with which she read and the fact that she was liable to forget details, and consequently she tended to avoid reading altogether. With the success of her son at school she had lived a moment of triumph, of deep well-being because her son's success was felt as her own.

I consistently interpreted to her that her material reflected a deep feeling of shame and her fear of exposing the shameful parts of herself to me in the analysis. Together with this, I consistently pointed out that she was showing me the frightened and panicky little girl inside herself who could not make sense of the complex events in the outside world. After this, she was able, for the first time, to acknowledge that she had very few memories of childhood. This had been quite a remarkable feature in this patient. Although her father had died when she was at college, she could scarcely remember him, and it was clear that she was very afraid of letting memories of the more distant past come into her mind. It was as if she was terrified of letting her mind wander while remembering. When I would ask her about something in the past or make some tentative link with her past, she would "freeze", and her mind would become quite blank.

Gradually, in the second year of her analysis, she could recall a few specific memories of her childhood that would "slip out" as associations. Although she would attempt to discard them as unimportant and irrelevant, it was evident that they were all linked with situations in which she was very frightened. For example, she remembered an excursion by car during which she was car-sick and terrified that the sick feeling would never end. Once, when she had run impetuously across an icy road, she had slipped and felt completely out of control. Riding a horse or a bicycle were continual sources of terror, and driving a car made her extremely anxious. I want to add that the extraction of details of events such as these required much perseverance on my part, as their appearance in consciousness would tend to be immediately wiped out. One could also add here her memories of being criticized, of being told not to frown, not to fidget, and so on.

She now became increasingly aware that weekends and holidays were very difficult for her. Quarrels at home reached a peak during breaks from the analysis, her children became "impossible", and her friends would be rejecting or disappointing. At first she only accepted the connection between these experiences and the breaks in the analysis on an intellectual level, and she would criticize herself for not yet having learned to cope with the weekends and holidays. She dismissed my suggestion that she might be missing me during these times as "ludicrous".

In the following year she was able to bring a relatively more coherent picture of her current life situation and, to some extent, of her past. What has emerged, among many other things, is the dominant theme of her having been unable to cope, from early in her life, with any situation in which she felt put under pressure of any sort. For a long time I had noticed that she constantly felt pushed and coerced by me. I also noticed that in my countertransference I had become increasingly irritable and impatient with her, and the realization of this allowed me to make a tentative reconstruction of her perception of her mother as someone who did not respond to her needs, who always seemed impatient and in a hurry. She was able to confirm this fully by a number of memories.

Mrs B. typically reacted to "pressure" by an overwhelming feeling of confusion and panic and would either "freeze" or rush immediately to comforting daydreams or to stereotyped patterns of behaviour, as if she were reaching out in a desperate and impulsive way for an object or situation that was safe and familiar. In this respect her anxieties and panic states were quite different in quality from those that I have experienced in the ordinary anxious or phobic patient in analysis. They were much more reminiscent of the panic of the child with stranger anxiety or of the organic patients with "catastrophic reactions" as described by Kurt Goldstein.[18]

I do not want to minimize the role of this patient's highly sadistic phantasies and her correlated fears of violence and assault. Certainly such phantasies and projections played an important part in her development and in her current state, but they are not what I wish to concentrate on here. Rather, I want to place emphasis on the *style* of her reaction to her anxiety rather than on its content or its cause.

One or two examples may be helpful here. Mrs B. had always been constipated, and she recalled her mother's rigid insistence that she perform on the lavatory before leaving the house. In this situation she could not pass a bowel motion at all. Even today she can only defecate on the days when she does not work and can take her time. This pattern of "freezing up" is also reflected in her analysis. When she panicked if I pressed her in any way for further material or for clarification, she had to be gently coaxed in order to restore her equilibrium. For instance, when I sensed that she was running away from the perception of a frightening aspect of herself, I would very often find myself saying, "You know, you will need to make friends with this child part of yourself, but we have plenty of time." Such comments always seemed to help her, but I think that it would be a mistake to understand this pattern of reaction in the patient *purely* in terms of anal-retentive impulses and phantasies.

Similarly, her learning and reading difficulties at school could be understood in terms of her panic at being confronted with a task that she did not immediately know how to solve, where the answer was not immediately familiar or obvious. In these circumstances she had been unable even to listen to what the teacher was saying, and this was repeated in the analysis. Throughout her life Mrs B. had experienced difficulty in learning through problem-solving, through tolerating uncertainty even for a moment. This was extremely limiting and had always been a source of profound humiliation. On the other hand, she overvalued the type of learning that involved changing her self-representation by direct and active imitation and saw the analysis as a process whereby she would be taught and could copy techniques for improving herself, for bettering her self-image. This added substantial difficulties to her analysis, but eventually she showed a greater degree of comfort with herself and began to accept the reality of an inner psychic life, of phantasies, wishes, and urges as distinct from actions or deeds. She was more able to tolerate the dissonance of the strange and moved towards the tenuous establishment of a "good-enough" self-representation with a consequent increase in her feelings of trust.

I end the description of Mrs B.'s analysis at this point, and I hope that by now some idea will have been gained of the sort of connection that can be made between this patient's reactions and what I have said earlier about stranger anxiety. Certainly the description of this patient must give rise to thoughts that she is someone who has been chronically afraid of her projected sadistic wishes; who is perhaps tormented by masochistic impulses; who suffers from acute and primitive guilt feelings arising from the persecutory introjects that form her superego and contain and deflect her own aggressive impulses; who is constantly ashamed because of her exhibitionistic desires and feelings of castration; who is afraid of death and mutilation; who fears the loss of control of her sphincters; or who suffers from acute separation anxiety, compounded by her own projected hostility, resulting in the fear of the loss of the ambivalently loved mothering object. All of this has, in some way, emerged in the analytic work, but equally all of this is, in my view, subordinate to a fear of experiencing or of re-experiencing a particular active state of being catastrophically overwhelmed when confronted with the unfamiliar.

This patient differed from the more usual neurotic patient in that any interpretation regularly caused panic instead of providing a feeling of relief. One could say that the interpretations, however correct, aroused the danger that she might be faced with a strange and unfamiliar aspect of herself and of the object, and that this was a particularly intolerable threat for her. Even the process of free association represented a threat. As a result, she would rush to say something—usually something logically disconnected with what she had been saying previously, very often a piece of intellectualization—simply because it reflected her familiar, recognizable self at which she could clutch. At the same time, she could turn to me as a familiar (and therefore safe) "approving" object. It was not even necessary for me to interpret some unconscious wish, conflict, thought, or phantasy for a panic reaction to occur.

Mrs B. had to cling rigidly to a picture of herself as a capable, solicitous, caring person, and she made strenuous and continuing efforts to dissociate strange, threatening, and unwanted thoughts, wishes, and feelings from herself, so that she could feel herself to be neither aggressive nor helpless. She also sought aspects of her own self that she saw in others whom she could admire, so that she could additionally feel close to herself by relating to others who were extensions of herself. I think that my feeling of confusion in the countertransference was in part due to this. In addition, Mrs B. clung to an image of a highly idealized, powerful, and perfect object, which she then felt she could woo to obtain praise, closeness, and affirmation. In many respects this object represented her maternal grandmother, but also her mother. This phantasied object was constantly externalized, particularly in the transference, but was also identified with. So she often tried to mould me into the all-powerful, all-knowing object who would approve of her and whom she could imitate.

I want to emphasize again how different the picture presented by Mrs B. was from the one we normally see and expect in neurotic patients. It is true that she had to deal with many unconscious conflicts and resulting persecuting phantasies. She was dominated, too, by severe jealousy and envy. Yet her fears were not simply based on conflict and on integrated and organized projections or externalizations. Because they represented a constant and desperate apprehension that she could not keep herself safe from anything that might be strange and intrusive, she attempted to maintain a *defensive* phantasy of being a perfect child in close symbiotic unity with a perfect mother. Her fear of the strange was intimately linked with her fear of separateness—hence the tremendous need to preserve the state representing an ideal mother–child unity. Her attempts to create such a situation of union and "oneness" were most evident in the transference. Although she clung to her idealization of her own self and of the "good" object that would admire and comfort her and was dominated by a quite general feeling of apprehension that she tried to cover up in a variety of ways, it became clear that she was by no means psychotic or even "borderline". Her overriding fear was that her highly contrived illusion of oneness with the mother might be shattered by something that she could not immediately integrate into her experience, which would lead to panic and to feelings of isolation, to worthlessness and loss of control, so that she would be overcome by feelings of annihilation. Consequently, she suffered from a chronic anxiety that her defensive posture could not be maintained.

I commented earlier on the role of the refuelling dialogue, in which the infant scans the environment—including himself, for he is also part of his environment—for sensory and affective cues that can provide him with a sense of security. The creation of self- and object-representations in the infant are two sides of the same process, and at a certain phase this renders him particularly vulnerable because their development is associated with a growing sense of separateness. We know nowadays how important are the predictable, mutual signals in the mother–child dialogue for establishing organized and cohesive object- and self-representations. In all children, the fear of being overwhelmed by the dissonance of the strange and the consequent fear of loss of the mother is to a large extent overcome by the constant refuelling provided by scanning both mother and self. In the normal child, satisfactory experiences within the mother–child dyad create a feeling of basic trust and, as the infant becomes a toddler, the refuelling that he obtains bolsters his feeling of self-sufficiency and autonomy, so that he will gradually be able to separate from his mother and deal with his ambivalence and with new experiences without too much threat to his inner sense of security.

Some children, however, like my patient Mrs B., are so afraid of the dissonance consequent on perception of the strange that they have to cling to the mother, to scan her and their relationship to her, for frequent refuelling. They become intolerant of any change in her, in themselves, or in their relationship. They allow themselves, almost literally, very little "space" for movement and change. With further development, the restricted *external* situation that they have to create becomes increasingly internalized, and such children, I believe, re-establish the same situation of "limited space" *internally*. In this sense, one could say that they do not allow themselves sufficient psychic space in their inner world of representations to tolerate the new and the strange. Like Mrs B., they are terrified of experiencing overwhelming dissonance and panic and need to cling to idealized phantasy images of their objects and of themselves in order to obtain, in thought and phantasy, perceptual and affective consonance and refuelling. Their dialogue in phantasy with representatives of the idealized object and with the idealized self, with the "false object" and "false self", is compulsive and frequent, and they are terrified if it is disturbed by unwanted, unfamiliar, intrusive experiences. However, they will attempt to arrange the external world in which they live so that they can gain the illusion that this inner situation is maintained. Such patients are, of course, extremely egocentric, and an understanding of their functioning may provide a further dimension of understanding in the complicated topic of narcissism.

CHAPTER SEVEN

Comments on
the psychodynamics of interaction

Introduction

I n this chapter an attempt is made to show how the externalization of the unconscious phantasy derivatives of internal object
relationships by both analyst and patient can interact, making
it vital for the analyst to keep in touch with his countertransference. The need to use both one-person and two-person models in
order to understand such interaction is illustrated by a rather
graphic clinical example.

* * *

One of the major theoretical issues in considering processes of
interaction is the question of whether it is appropriate to use a one-
person or two-person frame of reference. This is a complicated
issue and one that cannot be answered simply by saying that the
psychoanalytic model of the mind is a one-person model on the
grounds that all information arising from the outside does so as
mental representations of one sort or another. Furthermore, it
could be said that the essence of the psychoanalytic point of view
is that these representations, and all our feelings, are profoundly

affected by what arises from the inside. In a paper some time ago[1] I suggested that the theoretical models, theories, or schemata used by psychoanalysts are not fully integrated with one another, and that there were significant differences between our private psychoanalytic theories and what I called the "public" or "official" theories of psychoanalysis. I suggested that the complex private preconscious working model of the psychoanalyst—essentially a set of not-very-well-integrated part-theories—had an important advantage over the public or "official" ones in that "such a loosely jointed theory . . . allows developments in psychoanalytic theory to take place without necessarily causing radical disruptions."

The point I wanted to underline there is that what was critical for our psychoanalytic thinking are those parts of the theories we use that relate to our work. This means that "for most of us the theory needs to be a clinically, psychopathologically, and technically oriented one, which also includes a central preoccupation, not only with the abnormal, but with the normal as well".

In fact, we use both a one-person and a multi-person (usually a two-person) model in our psychoanalytic thinking. We are nowadays particularly interested in the analyst–patient dyad, in analyst–patient and patient–analyst interaction, and here we undoubtedly make use of a two-person frame of reference as well as an intrapsychic one. We do not normally know when we switch from the one to the other; and I believe that this relatively automatic use of more than one model is greatly to our advantage. The analytically informed observer of the interpersonal interaction is, of course, primarily the analyst—and for control cases also the supervisor of the candidate's work. However, as I indicated earlier, from the point of view of the psychoanalytic model of the mind, our perspective is an intrapsychic one. Even so, we constantly move from one perspective to the other, translating the two-person viewpoint into an intrapsychic one and vice versa; and when we make reconstructions of the past, we do not restrict ourselves to intrapsychic processes, although they are a central consideration. Any reconstruction of the past that refers only to intrapsychic processes runs the risk of lacking an important dimension. In contrast, when we make *constructions* about the way the patient's mind works in the present, about its *current* structure and organization, the model is essentially intrapsychic: although I must say that this is not necessarily so, for some of our constructions refer to the way the individual relates to and reacts to others, and for this we, at times appropriately, use an interpersonal frame of reference. So here we have (and need) two broad frames of reference, which have a special and as yet not well-worked-out relationship.

In this connection, the concept of the representational world may be particularly useful. It has been compared to a stage set within a theatre.

> The characters on the stage represent the child's various objects, as well as the child himself. Needless to say, the child is usually the hero of the piece. The theatre, which contains the stage, would correspond to aspects of the ego, and the various functions such as scene-shifting, raising or lowering the curtain, and all the machinery auxiliary to the actual stage production would correspond to those ego functions of which we are not normally aware. Whereas the characters on the stage correspond . . . to self and object representations, their particular form and expression at any one point in the play correspond to self and object images.[2]

Some phantasies are, descriptively speaking, unconscious, while others are conscious. In the representational world the representations of self and object in conscious or unconscious phantasy can be distinguished from those that arise from perception of the external world and in our thoughts about the external world. The latter have a particular stamp of reality that distinguishes them from the content of conscious or preconscious phantasy. It follows that some self- and object-representations are, descriptively speaking, unconscious, while others are conscious; and subjective content that may be tolerable when unconscious may well be unacceptable to consciousness and needs to be defended against. In this connection it can be said that the various forms of projection and externalization involve different forms of *displacement* within the representational world, displacement of unwanted or unacceptable aspects of the current unconsciously phantasied self- or object-representation onto the representation of an external person (i.e. a person other than oneself)—perhaps it would be better to say *integrated* with the representation of a person.

This view of projection or externalization is embedded in a one-person psychology. Yet the description of externalization by many authors appropriately and inevitably involves more than such representational displacements—that is, it involves a two-person psychology. I refer here, for example, to what has been described by Anna Freud, in *The Ego and the Mechanisms of Defence*, as "altruistic surrender", or living through another person—that is, facilitating in another the gratification of unconscious wishes of one's own that have been surrendered in a so-called altruistic fashion. I would also refer to Melanie Klein's concept of projective identification[3] as it has been developed by her followers (Melanie Klein restricted the concept to a process occurring in unconscious phantasy.[4]) Here the most striking two-person formulation of projective identification is that given by Wilfred Bion,[5] who speaks in quite concrete terms of putting an aspect of the self into the object. In referring to the relation of the infant to its mother (and this is thought to be equally true of the patient and the analyst), he says:[6]

> An evacuation of the bad breast takes place through a realistic projective identification. The mother, with her capacity for reverie, transforms the unpleasant sensations linked to the "bad breast" and provides relief for the infant who then reintrojects the mitigated and modified emotional experience, i.e., reintrojects . . . a non-sensual aspect of the mother's love.

Wishes, whether instinctual or not, usually involve both self- and object-representations, and representations of the interaction between the two. If we take the view that the satisfaction of the wish comes about through the attainment of an *identity of perception*, we can see how the patient can subtly and unconsciously manipulate reality so as to gain a correspondence between what is perceived and what is wished for. This can still be understood in terms of a one-person psychology, since the awareness of reality is mediated through conscious and unconscious perception. It is appropriate to say that what we get when we interact with reality are changes in the representational world, in particular that part of the representational world that is geared to external reality. So, for example, if we have a patient who is guilty over some internally forbidden wish—particularly an unconscious transference wish—then he may deal with this by provoking the analyst into being angry with him, in order to relate to an *external* critic rather than to an internal one. This provocation, this manipulation of the analyst, is in one sense a two-person process, but in another sense it is part of a one-person psychology, since the manipulative process is based on the subject's activity directed towards a perceived object, this activity being adjusted and modulated on the basis of consciously or unconsciously perceived "feedback".

So far we have only looked at one side of the process of externalization—that is, actualization. In this context one can draw on the idea of the "role-responsiveness" of the analyst, a process that is largely unconscious, that contributes to the countertransference and is ideally noticed by the analyst when his "free-floating responsiveness" exceeds appropriate limits. The actual interventions of the analyst obviously have a profound effect on the patient, and here the analyst's personality and psychic structure play a major role. For example, analysts, through appropriate interpretations, can convey, to varying degrees, an attitude of tolerance and a feeling of safety within the analytic situation. Unfortunately some analysts do just the opposite, reinforcing the patient's superego by their comments (often this activity is quite unconscious on the analyst's part). However, in a well-conducted analysis, the patient can identify with the analyst's tolerance of unconscious infantile wishes, and this can reduce conflict and consequently have a moderating effect on some of the patient's symptoms. Few people now subscribe to the idea that the analyst is a "mirror", and even if he is an analyst who is most attentive to the analytic "rules" and who adheres strictly to the analytic "frame", he will constantly and inevitably be conveying his own personality to the patient. Much of the patient's appreciation of this will be unconscious, but we have to accept that this is part of what normally goes on in analysis. No two analysts and no two analyses are the same. What is important here, with regard to the analyst's own normal countertransference and his own unresolved problems, is his need to scan his own behaviour, thoughts, and phantasies from time to time during the session and to evaluate their relevance to what is occurring in the session. This is a tall order, of course, and not always easy to carry out successfully.

An example, which points to how complicated the interaction between patient and analyst can be, might be useful here.*

> This is the case of a young accountant in his twenties, who was in analysis with a male analyst. Everything went well in the analysis for some time, and the analyst told his colleagues of his brilliant and insightful patient. After about a year of analysis the patient announced his wish to marry his girlfriend, who had become pregnant. The analyst did not interpret the patient's resistance to his affectionate homosexual transference towards his analyst and the need to defend against the associated homosexual anxieties, but he believed that the patient's wish to marry was an unacceptable piece of acting-out. The analyst felt that this created an analytic impasse and said that the analysis would be stopped if the patient proceeded with the marriage. Nevertheless, the patient went ahead and married. His analyst did not, in fact, stop the analysis, but from that point on his attitude towards his patient changed markedly. The patient felt quite sure that the analyst did not like him and complained to his friends that his analyst was constantly critical and rejecting in his attitude.

> In time the patient's wife was experiencing a threatened miscarriage. The patient was very preoccupied with this, and the analyst expressed the view that while the patient was so anxious about a real external situation, there was not much point in his being analysed, and he ended the analysis. Of course it is easy to say that this represented a piece of acting-out in the analyst's countertransference, and this was indeed the case. However, it is worth examining the interaction between patient and analyst in a little more detail. On the one hand, the patient wanted to be the most loved patient of his analyst, repeating wishes he had towards his own father, with whom he had had a warm and affectionate relationship until the birth of a sister

---

*The material on which this example is based was available to me because of my intimate knowledge of the analyst involved, and because I had the opportunity to analyse the patient some years later.

when the patient was about six. After that the patient felt that the father had shifted his affections to the little girl, and he felt abandoned and rejected. One could say that the analyst responded fully to the role that the patient had unconsciously evoked in him, repeating in his role-responsiveness a childhood experience of the patient. On the other hand, we have some interesting information about what went on in the analyst. Some twenty years previously, the analyst's wife had become pregnant with her first child. The analyst was extremely excited by this and looked forward to having a son or daughter—something he had wanted for a long time. However, he discovered that he was not the father of the child; he was hurt and angry and demanded a divorce. The wife pleaded with him to divorce her only once the child was born, as she was desperate that the child should have a name and be born in wedlock. He agreed to this, but after the child's birth rejected both the wife and the baby and had no contact with them afterwards. Subsequently he married again.

It seems probable that the analyst enacted, with his young patient, the same initial enthusiasm followed by disappointment at the patient's unfaithfulness, and then rejected—in a sense divorced—him. The patient was also the disappointing son who had to be disowned. It seems that what occurred here was a complex transference–countertransference interaction, a scenario that had, so to speak, two separate scripts that fitted each other well and in which both patient and analyst played a part. It is impossible to disentangle the relative roles played by each of the two leading actors in this little analytic drama. The patient later went on to have further analysis, which appeared to be beneficial.

There is another aspect to all of this that is worth mentioning. Ernst Ticho has written of the life-goals of the patient,[7] and we can add that the analyst also has life-goals, ambitions, aspirations, and so on. If the life-goals and the social value systems of the patient and the analyst are the same, then we have a matrix within which the analysis is conducted that is, I believe, intrinsically unanalysable, as it is not a source of conflict.[8] If the transference of the patient fits with the countertransference of the analyst and the analyst does not gain insight into this, then we have an equally potentially unanalysable area. In this connection the way in which the narcissistic needs of both analyst and patient are structured plays an important role, and it is vital that the analyst be aware of the details of these needs in himself as well as in his patient.

CHAPTER EIGHT

A theory of
internal object relations

Introduction

I n the previous chapters a number of ideas relating to the development of object relationships were considered, with special reference to the role of feeling states in that development. It was pointed out that the term "object relationship" has a variety of meanings, and that there is a need to face the task of integrating the theory of object relationships into the intrapsychic psychology of psychoanalysis. The notion of an object relationship as the energic investment of an object was criticized, and it was emphasized that the relationship between two people frequently involved an interchange of very subtle and complicated cues. Each partner in the relationship can be regarded as having, at any one time, a particular role for the other, pressures being placed on the other in order to obtain a particular type of response.

This chapter gives an account of our attempt to come to terms with the concept of internal object relations and to find a place for it within acceptable psychoanalytic theory. We have put forward the view that the internal object can be regarded as a structure outside the realm of conscious or unconscious subjective experience, a structure built up during the individual's development and strongly influenced by the child's subjective perceptions and phantasies. The internal objects, in turn, influence perception, thought, phantasy, current object relations, transference, and many other aspects of experience and behaviour. In the work of analysis, the concepts of internal object and internal object relation act as useful organizing constructs for both analyst and patient.

Many different expectations, feelings, wishes, and thoughts are involved in interpersonal interaction and can be discerned in any continuing relationship between two people. This holds for object relationships in phantasy as well as for relationships with "external" persons, and while the interaction in phantasy may not always be as satisfying, it does allow for greater control of the relationship in a wish-fulfilling way. So the object relationship is seen as an intrapsychic one, depicted in conscious or unconscious subjective experience by phantasy representations. The object plays as important a role as the self in the mental representations that form the wish or wishful phantasy. Indeed, it is the interaction between self- and object-representations that is of the greatest importance. The notion of wish should not, in this context, be restricted to instinctual wishes; it includes wishes to maintain well-being, safety, and feelings of being in control. Moreover, a powerful motivational force is the need to defend against unpleasant feelings or against the anticipation of such feelings. There is also constant pressure to replenish supplies of well-being, security, and self-esteem. These can be gained by interaction with the object in reality or by means of phantasy. Object relations can, from this point of view, be seen as wish-fulfilments, the wish being fulfilled through the finding of an appropriately responding object in reality or in phantasy. This experience provides an "identity of perception" in the fulfilment of the wish, an identity that may be disguised and therefore conceal the underlying unconscious wish. The striving for object-related wish-fulfilment as described above is clearly shown in the transference situation.

* * *

The theory of internal object relationships and its clinical application has often been difficult to discuss because of the lack of clarity about what constitutes an object relations theory. There are many theories that contain, as central elements, ideas and formulations about object relationships; indeed, from early on there was a definite, albeit very simple, object relations theory in classical Freudian psychoanalysis. But considerable development has taken place, beginning with Karl Abraham, Sandor Ferenczi, Ronald Fairbairn, and Melanie Klein. In Klein's work, particularly on the early development of conscience in the child,[1] the concept of the "internalized" object was present from the outset. What we aspire to do here is to present a particular *perspective* on internal object relations and to look at some aspects of the clinical situation from this perspective.

In Freud's writings the early notion of what we can call "internal objects" was that of objects of the past revived in the transference. In *Studies on Hysteria*, Freud had referred to transference as a "false connection" between someone who had been the object of the patient's earlier wishes and the doctor now treating the patient. In order to have such a "false connection" between the past and the present, the object of the earlier wishes must have been internalized. Throughout Freud's writings, there are references to the objects of the drives, to object imagos, objects in conscious daydreams or in unconscious phantasy, and objects that played a major role in the formation of the ego, the ego ideal, and the superego. Freud commented in *The Ego and the Id* that "the character of the ego is a precipitate of abandoned object-cathexes and contains the history of those object-choices", and regarding the superego we have his final statement in *An Outline of Psychoanalysis*, summarizing his views. He wrote:

> a portion of the external world has . . . been abandoned as an object and has instead, by identification, been taken into the ego and thus become an integral part of the internal world. This new psychical agency continues to carry on the functions which have hitherto been performed by people [the abandoned objects] in the external world: it observes the ego, gives it orders, judges it and threatens it with punishments, exactly like the parents whose place it has taken.

Beginning in the 1920s, Melanie Klein's work placed emphasis on ideas concerning internal objects, but she did not differentiate between these and the processes involved in the creation of a perceptual image of the object that could be revived in memory or in the conscious or unconscious phantasy life of the individual. Furthermore, these were not distinguished from the structuralization of an object as an internal authority figure, the model of the objects in the superego as described by Freud. (The meaning and value of the concept of "structure" has been somewhat ambiguous in the psychoanalytic literature.[2] The notion as used here does not refer to the "macrostructures" of id, ego, and superego.[3] We use the term in the sense of an enduring organization, which may or may not be involved in current mental processes to a significant extent but nevertheless persists and can be brought into use when appropriate.[4]) For this lack of differentiation Klein was roundly criticized by Edward Glover[5] in a violent attack on Kleinian formulations, in which he pointed out that Kleinian theory had extended Freud's concept of unconscious phantasy to cover *all* mental life and that consequently important theoretical distinctions had been lost. Moreover, Klein appeared to have allocated a substantial degree of autonomy to her internal objects, and Kleinian theory often sounds as if the internal objects have an independent life of their own. It is only fair to say, however, that the distinctions between perception, memory, and phantasy that Klein failed to make were not systematically made in the Freudian literature of the time. There was also no clear theoretical differentiation in the psychoanalytic literature between the various forms of internalization, and thus terms such as "identification", "introjection", "incorporation", and "internalization" tended to be used interchangeably.[6]

In the 1950s we began to work at the Hampstead Child Therapy Clinic (now the Anna Freud Centre), and the task offered to one of us (JS) was to attempt, with a group of colleagues, some clarification of the superego concept. This confronted the group with what we can call problems about internalization and the conceptual status of the introject or internal object.[7] The project was in the framework of what was called the Hampstead Psychoanalytic Index, which was a procedure in which items of clinical analytic material were classified under different headings, derived from psychoanalytic theory.

It soon became clear, in the work on the Index, that when the theoretical categories were applied to the child psychoanalytic material, in many cases the fit was not very good. The need became urgent to revise the theoretical formulations in some areas, so that they could better encompass the clinical material. So, for example, although it was easy to talk about "ego identifications" as opposed to "superego identifications", in practice it was often impossible to distinguish between the two.

The climate in the Hampstead Index Project was one in which it was recognized that parts of analytic theory did not fit well together; and also that there was a need for theoretical development.[8] Although the group saw itself as working within the mainstream of classical psychoanalytic theory, over the years it was possible to tolerate and sustain theoretical ambiguities and even contradictions. It should be said, however, that in the early days, probably because of group prejudices, Fairbairn's formulations did not appear useful to those of us working on the superego concept at the Hampstead Clinic; nor did Klein's ideas, which were difficult to assimilate into mainstream psychoanalytic theory, although we struggled to understand them. The notion of projective identification, which had been introduced by Melanie Klein[9] and which in Kleinian theory played a major part, along with the mechanisms of splitting and introjection, in determining the nature of internal objects, was equally difficult to assimilate. It appeared to non-Kleinians that the concept of projective identification was being used in a very concrete and ill-defined way. Nevertheless, these ideas were in the air, and we have no doubt that they exerted an influence on us, however intangible that influence may have been.

A significant step forward in psychoanalytic theorizing that had been made by Heinz Hartmann,[10] and by Edith Jacobson in her paper on "The Self and the Object World",[11] was of very great value in the work in the Index project. They distinguished between the ego as a structure and as the mental representation of the self. Freud's use in *The Ego and the Id* of the term *"das Ich"* for both ego and self had been extremely confusing, especially after the introduction of the structural theory, when the concept of ego partially changed meaning: it was now conceived of as a large-scale agency operating in the mind, although clearly something of its previous status remained. The distinction between ego as a structure and ego as a representation of the self, which paralleled the object-representation, allowed us to look back at Freud's writings and to retranslate such obscure phrases as that which described the ego as "first and foremost a body-ego" into the much more comprehensible notion that "the self representation is first and foremost a representation of a body-self". Moreover, the work of Hartmann and Jacobson allowed narcissism to be understood as the love for the self (or its mental representation). Love for the object could then be contrasted much more clearly with love for oneself than with love for the ego, which had come to be seen as a highly organized mental structure having a variety of functions.

It must have been in part the experience in the Hampstead Index and in the British Society that suggested the idea that as the analyst gains experience and competence, he will preconsciously (and therefore, in a descriptive sense, unconsciously) construct partial theories or models that can be used as appropriate. There is no problem about their contradicting one another—as long as they remain unconscious. Such partial theories can, however, become conscious in some form if they fit with "public" or "official" theory—if they can be made psychoanalytically plausible.[12]

The adoption of a "representational" point of view permitted a useful approach to be made to questions of object relationship.[13] Arlow[14] has pointed out that pre-representational approaches have led to substantial confusion, because they "disregard the fact that at all times we are dealing with a psychological experience, the mental representation of an object, a persistently 'internal' experience". It is important to add that the term "representation" can itself be a source of confusion, in that it relates to subjective experience on the one hand and to what can be called a non-experiential organization on the other. So, for example, self-representation can be a (conscious or unconscious) image, idea, or percept of oneself at a particular time, or a set of such experiences sharing a common identity. (The term "image" is not used here only in the sense of a visual experience. It applies to conscious or unconscious experiential data arising from all the sensory modalities, including proprioceptive or kinaesthetic experiences.) However, the term "self-representation" also refers to a non-experiential organization (structure), analogous to the body schema[15] or the body image.[16] The extension of the notion of the body schema to that of self-representations and object-representations has been discussed at some length elsewhere.[17] It was commented there that

From the concept of the self representation, which is not very much removed from the body schema, it is not a difficult step to make the further extension to representations that correspond to all the non-self components of the child's world. As the child gradually creates a self representation, so he builds up representations of others, in particular of his important love and hate objects. In the beginning, the representations that he constructs are those that are linked with need satisfaction, but he gradually creates schemata of many other things, activities and relationships. He does all of this as a consequence of the successive experiences of his own internal needs and their interaction with his external environment.

Based on the distinction between self- and object-representations, the work on the superego allowed a distinction to be made between various forms of internalization and made for more precision about the type of internalization that would be associated with superego formation—that is, which led to the formation of superego introjects. One differentiation is important for the present topic: that between identifications that modify the self-representation and those internalizations that were regarded as elevating certain object-representations to the special status of introjects. The two processes were referred to (somewhat arbitrarily) as "identification" and "introjection". Identification was seen as "a modification of the self representation on the basis of another (usually an object) representation as a model. . . . The representation used as a model in identification may, of course, be largely based on phantasy".[18] In contrast, introjection, in the sense in which it was used, was seen as the elevation of the object-representation to a special status—that of introject. We suggested that in the formation of the introject the object-representation would undergo a certain reorganization and be allocated an authority derived from that of the parents. In a sense it could be regarded as acting as a companion—perhaps, but not necessarily, a "superego companion"—that would exist in some way in the person's internal world but was not conceived of as part of that person's self-representation. In other words, if one *identified* with some aspect of a parent, then one would duplicate that perceived aspect in oneself and become more like that parent in some way. If one *introjected* the parent, then the introject would not directly modify one's self-representation but would become an internal companion, a sort of backseat driver. Of course we can—and frequently do—identify with the introject (that is, with the *representation* of the internal object), just as we might identify with an object perceived in the external world.

The important point here is not the terminology, nor even the theory evolved at the time, but the fact that these two mechanisms of "taking in" were conceived of as very different. The superego was seen as composed of introjects, which were regarded as having loving and supporting as well as criticizing functions.[19] Thus it seemed that the relationship between ego and superego could not only be regarded as that of an ego subservient to an internal critical agency, but it could also profitably be seen in object-relational terms.

It was, among many other influences, the increasing awareness in Britain of the possible usefulness of countertransference for understanding the unconscious material of the patient, the work on the development of object relationships in children by such observers as Margaret Mahler, and the increasing literature on object relationships coming from the United States that stimulated interest among many of us at the Hampstead Clinic in integrating the theory of object relationships—in particular internal object relations—into our psychoanalytic psychology. It had become clear to some of us that the conceptualization of an object relation in terms of the cathexis of the object with drive energy in one form or another was inadequate, and it was equally clear that another approach was necessary. This is an area that has preoccupied us for some time, and in recent years it has seemed that one approach might be based on the following points.

It is useful to consider first the relation of self- and object-representations to each other, on the one hand, and to the content of phantasies and wishes, on the other. *We can take the view that object relationships always involve an interaction between conscious or unconscious phantasy representations of self and object.* In memory and in thought, in conscious and unconscious phantasies and wishes, we do not get self- and object-representations in isolation, but in interaction. It was pointed out earlier that "every wish involves a self-representation, an object-representation, and a representation of the interaction between these". Furthermore, the notion of the

aim of an unconscious wish or of a wishful phantasy as the search
for gratification or the avoidance of unpleasure has to be reformu-
lated as the aim of a particular wished-for interaction between self
and other.

In a consideration of the metapsychology of phantasy,[20] a clear
distinction was found to be necessary, in the framework of Freud's
topographical theory, between unconscious phantasies in the
system *Unconscious* and those in the *Preconscious*. The latter are, of
course, unconscious in the descriptive sense. Preconscious phantasies can be seen in much the same way as conscious daydreams,
except that they are, descriptively speaking, unconscious. While
we use the term "wishful phantasy" in much the same way as
Freud did, we can distinguish, within the Preconscious system,
between the preconscious phantasy as a wish-fulfilment, on the
one hand, and as the content of an *unfulfilled* preconscious wish,
on the other. Both can be regarded as being in the experiential
realm, and both can (implicitly or explicitly) involve some form of
interaction between representations of self and object.

Whether or not we "place" such phantasies in the system Preconscious or in the unconscious ego of the structural theory (where
it would be a product of the ego function of phantasying), these are
phantasies that are formed *in the present*, and although to a large
extent they may be derivatives of the past, they are not entirely so.
They are current unconscious wishful phantasies, and it is the
further derivatives of these phantasies in consciousness or in action
that provide the analyst with relevant and significant clues to the
patient's phantasies and thoughts that exist just below the surface.
These include, of course, the conscious or unconscious transference
phantasies that the patient creates in the "here-and-now" of the
analysis, and which can then be addressed by the analyst.

In the wish-fulfilment that takes place through what one does
within oneself or to the external world, in what one does through
thought or overt action, *actualization* (see Chapters 2 and 3) comes
about through one's conscious or unconscious perception of the
effect of one's action—a perception that may be distorted to greater
or lesser extent. We can also have actualization through conscious
daydreaming and preconscious—therefore, descriptively speaking, unconscious—daydream phantasies, which achieve a gratifying effect through a *temporary partial suspension of the distinction*

between phantasy and reality—a distinction that can, in most people, be reinstated immediately when necessary. Of course, we cannot always succeed in the efforts to actualize our wishes, and if we fail to do so through reality or through daydreams and preconscious phantasies, we may have to find other ways—through dreams, delusions and other symptoms, creative productions, or various alternative compromise formations. It is worth emphasizing that much of what we call relations to external objects (and the transference in analysis) represents the fulfilment of preconscious wishful object-related phantasies.

Preconscious wishes may arouse conflict and are then defended against in one or other of a variety of ways. Some of these involve *transformations* and *displacements* of aspects of the self- and object-representations. So, from a representational point of view, projection or projective identification[21] *within the preconscious phantasy life of the individual* would involve a displacement of an aspect of the self-representation to the object-representation; similarly, identification would refer to a duplicating of some aspect of the object-representation in the representation of the self. Such manipulation of phantasy content with temporary suspension of the "hallmark of reality" is, of course, a characteristic aspect of phantasy construction.

The daydreams of childhood involve representations of self and of external objects—representations that are modified and distorted by a variety of defensive activities involving a process that can be called "representational displacement" (identification, all the varieties of projection, etc.). Modifications through representational displacement (from self to object, object to self, object to object, object to ideal self, etc.) occur in the area of the child's *perception* of the object, but they occur much more freely in the service of gratification and defence in the child's preconscious phantasy life. As the child develops, we get the creation of phantasy *themes* in which alternative sets of phantasy objects are created, and the experience of these new object-representations in the phantasy life of the young child contributes in turn to the world of structured internal objects.

We want to emphasize the distinction between the experiential content of a mental representation—the perceptual and ideational content—and the structural organization behind that content, which lies quite outside the realm of conscious or unconscious experience—unfortunately the term "representation" has been used for both in the psychoanalytic literature. The crucial distinction between the two meanings of representation was made—but not sufficiently—in the original work on the representational world,[22] although much emphasis was put on it some years later.[23] This is in line with the proposal (discussed in Chapter 4) that we can make a sharp conceptual differentiation between the "experiential" and the "non-experiential" parts of the mind. (Work by cognitive psychologists allows us to consider internal objects as being what we have called "dynamic templates". These are composed of "implicit" or "procedural" organizations, as opposed to the "explicit" ones that can be considered to compose unconscious phantasies.[24])

The psychoanalytic literature contains many valuable descriptions of how the infant gradually organizes and builds up mental representations of self and of important objects as a result of interaction with the external world. (In *Internal World and External Reality* Kernberg has given an excellent account of the way these processes occur.) The infant develops its capacity to distinguish between self and other, and to experience images in perception, memory, and gradually in phantasy—images of self and object and of the ways in which self and object interact. Although the images vary, each has a specific "signature" of identity for the child, and we can assume that the background non-experiential organizations structured by subjective experience are enduring ones, structures that in turn can affect perception, memory, and phantasy—indeed, the whole of the experiential realm—in various ways. (It seems likely, based on recent infant research, that there are predispositions in the baby for the early formation of specific structures.)

Obviously an intricate to-and-fro interaction must constantly be occurring between the experiential and non-experiential realms. The content of subjective experience, whether conscious or unconscious, must affect the organizations, structures, and processes within the non-experiential realm. Similarly, the non-experiential realm organizes and can be regarded as giving form to what is subjectively experienced. Perhaps the best example of this is the way in which non-experiential perceptual and cognitive structures, built up during development, modify the subjective data of experience as these are transformed into conscious and preconscious percepts. This is an essential part of the process of perception, in which perceptual "structures" are employed to give form to sensory data. Similarly, cognitive organizations in the non-experiential realm directly influence the form and subjective content of thought, including that special form of thought that we call phantasy.[25]

The internal objects created on the basis of childhood phantasy may in significant respects be radically different from the internalized experience of the objects of the person's childhood. We get a double layer of subjective experience in the formation of internal object relationships: on the one hand the child's experiences of reality, in particular of the actual interaction with the parents or parental figures, and on the other the conscious or preconscious phantasy formations as they develop and are defensively modified in the crucial childhood years. In turn, the internal object relationship as it exists in the non-experiential realm influences the content of the child's conscious or unconscious subjective experience, whatever form that experience might take.

A point needs to be made about *actualization* in relation to transference, object relations, and character traits. To the extent that the interaction between self- and object-representations is reflected in the ideational content of the wish, the attempt at actualization will often bring into play unconscious and subtle attempts to involve other persons to play the wish-fulfilling role. Nowhere is this seen more clearly than in the transference and in elements of the countertransference (although it should be emphasized that it is a grave error to assume that what the analyst becomes aware of as countertransference is always what the patient has "put into" the analyst. The result of such an assumption can only be "wild" countertransference analysis). In brief, the patient in the analytic situation may attempt to impose a role relationship on the analyst, and this form of externalization of an internal role relationship represents an integral part of the transference, just as it represents an integral part of object relationships in general. Many character traits can similarly be regarded as devices for provoking particular types of response in others, so that unconscious object-related wishes can be actualized and gratification achieved through the attainment of an identity of perception.

When we speak of gratification in this context we do not mean only pleasurable gratification—for example, wishes involving a need for punishment are frequently gratified in this way; the same is true for wishes to keep the object close and thus to avoid the pain of separation.

In the light of all of this, it seems most appropriate to restrict the term "internal objects" to refer to specific psychological structures that can be conceived of as lying outside the realm of subjective experience, and not to use it for conscious or unconscious self and object experiential representations. This is different from the Kleinian position, in which no distinction is made between the experiential and non-experiential realms. (We can consider the structures constituting internal objects and internal object relationships as being based on affectively invested "implicit" or "procedural" memories and organizations.[26])

It is not simply the child's conscious or unconscious *perception* of its interaction with the objects in the external world, however primitive or distorted that perception might be, which leads to the creation of the structures we call internal objects. Of the greatest importance is the influence of the child's phantasy life. With the growing development of the ego's defence mechanisms, self and object phantasy images are unconsciously manipulated by the ego by means of the ego function of phantasying,[27] sometimes in radical ways, to gain the fulfilment of wishes through actualization in phantasy as well as to maintain feelings of safety and well-being. We are all familiar with the way the child can deal simultaneously with hostile wishes and feelings of guilt by phantasying, in many different ways, battles between "goodies" and "baddies"—fights in which the "baddies" are defeated and the good people triumph. Of course we do this as adults as well, in a variety of ways—and this does not exclude psychoanalysts. We also have our cowboys and Indians, cops and robbers, Freudians and Kleinians or Kohutians. As psychoanalysts, we know that in such phantasies the "baddy" figures represent—one could say the representations are made to "contain"—unwanted or split-off aspects of the unconscious self-image that is felt to be bad, which arouses unconscious feelings of guilt, shame, or any other unpleasant affect and from which consciousness has to be protected.

These transformations—intrapsychic adaptations in the shape of splitting (in the sense of a splitting of a self- or object-representation), displacements, projections, and identifications—are compromise formations resulting from the ego's need to gratify unconscious wishes while simultaneously defending against them. These compromise formations in phantasy will inevitably follow certain themes—themes that change to some extent, but not entirely, as the child develops. To a certain degree these themes will be the product of the child's experience in interaction with the external object world, but to a significant extent they will reflect a consistency in the child's use of specific defence mechanisms. So if the child is a habitual user of identification with the aggressor, the phantasy themes and the objects represented in phantasy will frequently reflect identification with the aggressor. The same will be true if the child uses the mechanisms of changing passive into active, of reversal of roles, or of reaction formation—and there are always representations of an interaction between self and object involved. So, for example, in those people who use reaction formation as a defence, there are *always* accompanying critical thoughts about those other dirty, cruel, or exhibitionistic people onto whom the unacceptable impulse is projected. The phantasy relationship, conscious or unconscious, to those others with whom the person is *disidentified* is an important part of the reaction formation.

What we are leading up to here is that the structures that we call "internal objects" are in large part determined by the subjective experience of self–object interactions in the child's phantasy life. These structural organizations will to varying degrees reflect the characteristics of the parents. *However, they may in many respects be very different from the real parents as perceived by the child, because they are also to a marked degree the product of phantasies.* This is in line, of course, with Freud's observation in *An Outline of Psychoanalysis* that "It is a remarkable thing that the super-ego often displays a severity for which no model has been provided by the real parents".

It follows from this that internal objects, in the sense in which we have been using the term, will have been established well before the Oedipus complex has arrived on the scene. In this context it is appropriate, we believe, to speak of archaic elements in the superego, although we can expect major superimpositions on the system of pre-oedipal internalizations following the oedipal upheaval and the particular solutions to oedipal conflict found by the child.

Just as much as perception and phantasy contribute to the formation of internal objects, so the internal objects, in turn, contribute to the formation of wishful phantasies, to illusory perceptions, and in pathological states to delusions and hallucinations. The unconscious wishful phantasies find their gratification in all the varieties of "derivatives of the unconscious" through actualization and the attainment of a disguised identity of perception. As analytic practitioners, we are most concerned with the transference phantasies the patient brings to the analyst's consulting room and which he may attempt to gratify through some form of actualization in the analytic situation. We are referring here to what are, descriptively speaking, unconscious wishful phantasies, preconscious phantasies involving secondary process functioning, phantasies in the here-and-now that are not far from consciousness but are kept from reaching it by what Freud called the "second censorship" between the Preconscious and Conscious systems.[28] The patient will attempt to actualize these (descriptively) unconscious wishful phantasies, but the analyst has the possibility of interpreting them and bringing them to consciousness through the direct and indirect allusions to the transference in the patient's associations, through observation of the patient's behaviour, and through the scrutiny of countertransference thoughts, feelings, phantasies, and attitudes towards the patient.

Thus far we have referred to the concepts of internal object and internal object relationship as structures in the non-experiential realm that give rise to conscious or unconscious phantasies. These non-experiential structures, which can never be called into conscious or unconscious subjective experience, can nevertheless be considered to give form to conscious and unconscious phantasies in the experiential realm, as well as to other so-called "derivatives of the unconscious"—parapraxes, works of art, and the like.

In this context it should be remembered that the internal object is an organizing *construct* in the mind of the analyst, one that is of great value both to the theoretician and to the clinician. In the analytic situation all the analyst can see or know are the thoughts, phantasies, feelings, and behaviour of the patient as brought in, one way or another, by the patient, and the analyst can be aware of his own reactions to this material. While all this may be *perceived* by the analyst, the internal objects and internal object relationships, in the sense in which we have been describing them, can only be *conceived* of as organizations of some sort *lying behind* the material brought by or elicited from the patient. So when we speak of "internal objects" or "internal object relationships", we speak of *constructions* made by the analyst, which may then be conveyed to the patient in order to anchor the material elicited by the analytic work within an appropriate and fitting frame of reference—as with references to an "internal critic" of one sort or another and to the development and current functional interaction with that internal object.

The internal object, as it has been understood here, is evident only in the shape of its derivatives. So what is perceived by analyst and patient is *referred* to the hypothetical internal object in its relation to, and interaction with, the patient's own self. This construction is of the greatest value to both analyst and patient because, if it is both affectively and cognitively appropriate—if the patient understands it and feels that it is right—it becomes part of an extended view of the patient's own self and of his internal world, a view that is indispensable for the development of what we know as "analytic insight".

Let us illustrate what we mean. A patient brings a report that he was afraid when a policeman stopped his car, sure that he had done something seriously wrong, but the policeman only wanted to tell him that he needed to have a rear light repaired. He tells of receiving a letter from the tax authorities and panicking before opening it at the thought of the tax evasions he might be accused of and the penalties he would face. He brings several similar reports, and the analyst is able to convey to the patient how afraid he is of being accused of some awful misdeed by the analyst. From material such as this, with its obvious recurring theme, the analyst may eventually *construct* a notion of a threatening internal object that is externalized in a variety of situations. Furthermore, if the material supports it, the analyst may *conceive* of the relation of the patient to this internal object as not only one in which the patient feels frightened and guilty, but also one in which a sado-masochistic tie is involved in the relation to the internal object; equally, it may be appropriate at some point to indicate how the patient's own aggressive wishes are in some way embodied in the internal object. Above all, the analyst's conception of the internal object and the patient's interrelationship with it must relate to the *function* of that object in the patient's inner life and in his or her psychopathology.

We have spoken here of *constructions* and would differentiate these from reconstructions of the past. It is convenient to use the term "construction" to refer to the way in which the current internal world of the patient is organized, and "reconstruction" for what happened and what was experienced during development, as seen from the viewpoint of the analyst. Clearly there is an intimate relationship between construction and reconstruction, but the two do need to be differentiated, if only because of what Hartmann has called the "genetic fallacy" and the "change of function" of ego apparatuses.[29]

The terms "construction" and "reconstruction" have often been used synonymously, but it is useful to understand "construction" as relating to the role of the analyst in the analytic process and "reconstruction" as a shared activity of the analyst and the patient. In this context we should like to suggest that construction relates to the creation by the analyst of meaningful insights into the *current* inner world of the patient. So not only do we reconstruct the past, but as analysts we construct, for example, the internal object relationships of the patient and the mechanisms of defence used. Such constructions are not memories that have come to the surface through appropriate interpretation. They are interpretations (in the broadest sense of the term) of the significant and relevant aspects of the structure and function of the patient's mind. We make such constructions to increase the patient's insight and to expand his knowledge of himself and his inner world. So, for example, the patient may bring experiences of being warmly attracted to another person, this attraction being followed, after a few weeks, by disappointment and disillusionment. This pattern may show itself again and again and be repeated in the here-and-now of the transference. We construct from all this material, and from the patient's recollections of similar patterns of experience, the notion of an internal object and an internal object relationship. It should be emphasized that this is not a reconstruction of the past, although it may fit well with what we know and discover of the patient's past. It is a *new* formulation that allows the patient to have meaningful insight into how he or she functions in the present. Because of the process of development that has occurred since the early months and years, what we construct does not necessarily reflect exactly the structure of the child's mind as it was in infancy.

The problem of differentiating constructions from reconstructions becomes acute when we consider that the idea of transference has had to be extended in recent years to include the externalization of *internal* object relationships as well as repetitions of the past. It has become increasingly clear that we cannot consider the internal object as a simple internalization of an external object, even if we say that it is an external object as experienced by the child. The internal object can be radically modified by the child's phantasies and by all sorts of defensive activities occurring while creating these phantasies, including those subsumed under the headings of splitting and projective identification. These internal object relationships, based on relationships towards phantasy figures, may be very different from the perceived and recalled actual relationships of the patient to the important figures of early childhood. Evidently, emphasis needs to be placed on the reconstruction of the *phantasies* as well as of the perceived events of the past, but this is, of course, not at all an easy task.

As far as *reconstruction* is concerned, we can, very occasionally, get confirmatory memories from the early past through a reconstruction offered to the patient, but this does not occur all that often. It frequently happens that memories are evoked from the latency years, after the age of four or five, and as analysts we have the habit of taking the memories of childhood from the later age and dating them backwards, pushing them back in time as if they were early experiences. The memories from the first few years, before the so-called infantile amnesia, are very fragmentary and scattered. They are probably far fewer than is generally believed, in terms of what can be recalled with any precision.[30] More frequently recalled are memories that have been reorganized or early events told to the patient by relatives. The main aim of reconstruction is, as we see it, the anchoring of the analyst's understanding and constructions of the present in the past, so that the present— particularly the present as shown in the transference—once analysed, can be understood in terms of the past. *This provides a temporal dimension in the patient's view of himself.* However, the main aim of the work is not to discover what went on in the past, in order to release the repressed material (although such release may be a sign that the analysis is progressing), but to get a picture of the relevant aspects of the past so as to discover and understand better the present psychic structure and conflicts of the patient. This present psychic structure is intimately connected with the internal object relationships.

The world of phantasy objects differs markedly from the current real world as we know it (although the real world influenced its development in childhood), and the gap between the two is a very substantial source of tension. We are strongly motivated to bring the two worlds together as far as possible and to find ways of performing the difficult task of living simultaneously in both worlds. One way to do this is to draw on our capacity for phantasy, conscious and unconscious, and to amalgamate both worlds in our phantasy life; a more extreme way is to make a psychotic adaptation by means of delusions and hallucinations. If we can find objects in the real world onto whom we can externalize aspects of our internal objects, we will do so; we will actualize aspects of our internal world and will make use of our capacity for rationalization to make the amalgamation of the two as plausible as possible. This capacity for rationalization is, of course, a most highly developed human attribute.

We can best see this process of amalgamation of the two worlds in the transference situation, where the analyst holds back in order to allow the patient to distort his or her perception of the analyst and to try to evoke object-related role responses that belong to the patient's internal object relationships. It is a prime situation in which the patient can bring his two worlds together, and we are all aware of the ingenuity with which this can be done. In the analytic situation the patient unpacks the object aspects of his mental furniture, so to speak, and tries to place this furniture so that it seems as if it belongs and is appropriate.

Fairbairn, who placed great emphasis on internal object relationships in his theory, once remarked that

> in a sense, psycho-analytical treatment resolves itself into a struggle on the part of the patient to press-gang his relationship with the analyst into the closed system of the inner world

through the agency of transference, and a determination on the part of the analyst to effect a breach in this closed system and to provide conditions under which in the setting of a therapeutic relationship, the patient may be induced to accept the open system of outer reality.[31]

Fairbairn's "press-ganging" is, of course, the attempt to gratify unconscious wishes or wishful phantasies through actualizing them in the transference. We could say that it represents the externalization of internal object relationships, but strictly speaking it should be considered as the actualization of current (descriptively) unconscious phantasies derived from, or based on, the structured internal object relationships in the non-experiential realm.

A source of severe resistance in analysis, one that often leads to a negative therapeutic reaction, is our need to cling to the internal objects we have constructed. In this context it is perhaps appropriate to end this book by recalling the words of Byron's "The Prisoner of Chillon", relating to what he felt when set free.

> And thus when they appeared at last,
> And all my bonds aside were cast,
> These heavy walls to me had grown
> A hermitage—and all my own!
> And half we felt as they were come
> To tear me from a second home.

NOTES

Preface

1. P. King & R. Steiner (Eds.), *The Freud–Klein Controversies 1941–1945* (London: Routledge, 1991).
2. S. Freud, *An Outline of Psycho-Analysis*, in: *Standard Edition*, 23 (London: Hogarth, 1940a [1938]/1953–74).

Chapter 1

1. J. Sandler, "The background of safety", in: J. Sandler (Ed.), *From Safety to Superego* (New York: Guilford; London: Karnac Books, 1960/1987).
2. J. Sandler, "On the repetition of early childhood relationships in later psychosomatic illness", in: *The Nature of Stress Disorder*, Proceedings of a Conference of the Society for Psychosomatic Research (London: Hutchinson, 1959); "Unconscious wishes and human relationships", in: J. Sandler (Ed.), *Dimensions of Psychoanalysis* (London: Karnac Books, 1978/1989; Madison CT: International Universities Press, 1989).
3. J. Sandler, "On the concept of superego", in: *From Safety to Superego* (1960/1987).

4. J. Sandler, "Psychology and psychoanalysis", in: *From Safety to Superego* (1962/1987).

5. J. Sandler, & B. Rosenblatt, "The concept of the representational world", in: *From Safety to Superego* (1962/1987).

6. J. Sandler, A. Holder, & D. Meers, "The ego ideal and the ideal self", in: *From Safety to Superego* (1963/1987).

7. J. Sandler & W. G. Joffe, "On skill and sublimation", in: *From Safety to Superego* (1966/1987).

8. J. Sandler & W. G. Joffe, "Notes on childhood depression", *International Journal of Psycho-Analysis*, 46 (1965): 88–96; W. G. Joffe & J. Sandler, "Notes on pain, depression, and individuation", in: *From Safety to Superego* (1965/1987).

9. S. Freud, "On narcissism: an introduction", in: *Standard Edition, 14* (London: Hogarth, 1914c/1953–74).

10. Joffe & Sandler, "Notes on pain, depression and individuation".

11. W. G. Joffe & J. Sandler, "Some conceptual problems involved in the consideration of disorders of narcissism", in: *From Safety to Superego* (1967/1987).

12. S. Freud, *Inhibitions, Symptoms and Anxiety*, in: *Standard Edition, 20* (London: Hogarth, 1926d [1925]/1953–74).

13. W. G. Joffe & J. Sandler, "Adaptation, affects and the representational world", in: *From Safety to Superego* (1968/1987).

14. J. Sandler, "Psychological conflict and the structural model: some clinical and theoretical implications", *International Journal of Psycho-Analysis*, 55 (1974): 53–62.

15. J. Sandler & A.-M. Sandler, "On the development of object relationships and affects", *International Journal of Psycho-Analysis, 59* (1978): 285–296.

16. A. Freud, *The Ego and the Mechanisms of Defence* (London: Hogarth Press, 1936 [reprinted London: Karnac Books, 1993]).

17. J. Sandler, with A. Freud, *The Analysis of Defense* (New York: International Universities Press, 1985).

18. S. Freud, *The Ego and the Id*, in: *Standard Edition, 19* (London: Hogarth, 1923b/1953–74).

19. E. Kris, "Problems in clinical research: discussion remarks", *American Journal of Orthopsychiatry, 17* (1947): 210–214.

20. M. Schur, *The Id and the Regulatory Principles of Mental Functioning* (New York: International Universities Press, 1966).

21. S. Freud, *Beyond the Pleasure Principle*, in: *Standard Edition, 18* (London: Hogarth, 1920g/1953–74).

22. M. S. Mahler, F. Pine, & A. Bergman, *The Psychological Birth of the Human Infant* (New York: Basic Books, 1975 [reprinted London: Karnac Books, 1991]).

Chapter 2

1. S. Freud, *The Interpretation of Dreams*, in: *Standard Edition*, 4–5 (London: Hogarth, 1900a/1953–74).
2. S. Freud, "The neuro-psychoses of defence", in: *Standard Edition*, 3 (London: Hogarth, 1894a/1953–74); "Further remarks on the neuro-psychoses of defence", in: *Standard Edition*, 3 (London: Hogarth, 1896b/1953–74).
3. Freud, *The Ego and the Id*.
4. Freud, *Inhibitions, Symptoms and Anxiety*.
5. S. Freud, *The Origins of Psycho-Analysis: Letters to Wilhelm Fliess, Drafts and Notes* (London: Imago, 1897–1902/1954).
6. S. Freud (with J. Breuer), *Studies on Hysteria*, in: *Standard Edition*, 2 (London: Hogarth, 1896b/1953–74).
7. For a further discussion of these processes, see J. Sandler, A. Holder, C. Dare, & A. U. Dreher, *Freud's Models of the Mind: an Introduction* (London: Karnac Books, 1997; Madison CT: International Universities Press, 1997).
8. S. Freud, "Formulations on the two principles of mental functioning", in: *Standard Edition*, 12 (London: Hogarth, 1911b/1953–74).
9. Sandler, "Psychological conflict and the structural model".
10. O. F. Kernberg, "Self, ego, affects and drives", *Journal of the American Psychoanalytic Association*, 30 (1982): 893–917; see also *Object Relations Theory and Clinical Psychoanalysis* (New York: Jason Aronson, 1976).
11. J. Sandler & H. Nagera, "The metapsychology of fantasy", in: *From Safety to Superego* (1965/1987).
12. S. Freud, "Fragment of an analysis of a case of hysteria", in: *Standard Edition*, 7 (London: Hogarth, 1905e [1901]/1953–74).
13. Sandler & Nagera, "The metapsychology of fantasy".
14. A.-M. Sandler, "Comments on the significance of Piaget's work for psychoanalysis", *International Review of Psycho-Analysis*, 2 (1975): 365–378.
15. Freud, *The Interpretation of Dreams*; S. Freud, "The unconscious", in: *Standard Edition*, 14 (London: Hogarth, 1915e/1953–74).
16 J. Sandler & W. G. Joffe, "Towards a basic psychoanalytic model", in: *From Safety to Superego* (1969/1987).
17. Sandler, Holder, Dare, & Dreher, *Freud's Models of the Mind*.
18. J. Sandler, "Sexual phantasies and sexual theories in childhood", in: *Studies on Child Psychoanalysis: Pure and Applied* (New Haven, CT: Yale University Press, 1970).
19. Sandler, "The background of safety"; "On the concept of superego".
20. Sandler & Joffe, "Towards a basic psychoanalytic model".
21. Sandler & Nagera, "The metapsychology of fantasy".

22. S. Isaacs, "The nature and function of phantasy", *International Journal of Psycho-Analysis, 29* (1948): 73–97.
23. Freud, "Formulations on the two principles of mental functioning".
24. Sandler & Joffe, "On skill and sublimation".
25. J. Sandler, M. Kawenoka, L. Neurath, B. Rosenblatt, A. Schnurmann, & J. Sigal, "The classification of superego material in the Hampstead Index", *The Psychoanalytic Study of the Child, 17* (1962): 107–127; M. Wangh, "The 'evocation of a proxy': A psychological maneuver, its use as a defense, its purposes and genesis", *The Psychoanalytic Study of the Child, 17* (1962): 451–469.

Chapter 3

1. J. Sandler, C. Dare, & A. Holder, *The Patient and the Analyst* (London: Karnac Books, 1973; New York: International Universities Press. 1973; second, revised edition 1992).
2. Ibid.
3. P. Heimann, "On counter-transference", *International Journal of Psycho-Analysis, 31* (1950): 81–84; "Counter-transference", *British Journal of Medical Psychology, 33* (1960): 9–15.
4. Heimann, "On counter-transference".
5. D. W. Winnicott, "Countertransference", *British Journal of Medical Psychology, 33* (1960): 17–21.
6. This theme is developed in J. Sandler, "Reflections on developments in the theory of psychoanalytic technique", *International Journal of Psycho-Analysis, 73* (1992): 189–198.
7. Sandler, Holder, Dare, & Dreher, *Freud's Models of the Mind*.
8. J. Sandler (Ed.), *Projection, Identification, Projective Identification* (New York: International Universities Press; London: Karnac Books, 1987).
9. J. Sandler, "Countertransference and role-responsiveness", *International Review of Psycho-Analysis, 3* (1976): 43–47.

Chapter 4

1. See Sandler & Joffe, "On skill and sublimation"; Joffe & Sandler, "Some conceptual problems involved in the consideration of disorders of narcissism".
2. R. A. Spitz, *A Genetic Field Theory of Ego Formation* (New York: International Universities Press, 1959); *The First Year of Life* (New York: International Universities Press, 1965).
3. D. W. Winnicott, "Transitional objects and transitional phenomena", *International Journal of Psycho-Analysis, 34* (1953): 89–97; "The theory of the parent–infant relationship", *International Journal of Psycho-*

Analysis, 41 (1960): 585–595; *Playing and Reality* (London: Tavistock, 1971).

4. Mahler, Pine, & Bergman, *The Psychological Birth of the Human Infant.*

5. J. Bowlby, *Attachment and Loss. Vol. 1. Attachment* (London: Hogarth Press, 1969); *Attachment and Loss. Vol. 2. Separation, Anxiety and Anger* (London: Hogarth Press, 1973).

6. See, for example, L. J. Stone, H. T. Smith, & L. B. Murphy (Eds.), *The Competent Infant* (London: Tavistock, 1974); E. N. Rexford, L. W. Sander, & T. Shapiro, (Eds.), *Infant Psychiatry* (New Haven, CT: Yale University Press, 1976); R. N. Emde, "Development terminable and interminable. I. Innate and motivational factors from infancy", *International Journal of Psycho-Analysis, 69* (1988): 23–42; D. N. Stern, *The Interpersonal World of the Infant* (New York: Basic Books, 1985 [reprinted London: Karnac Books, 1998]); D. N. Stern, *The Motherhood Constellation* (New York: Basic Books, 1995 [reprinted London: Karnac Books, 1998]); T. B. Brazelton & H. Als, "Four early stages in the development of mother–child interaction", *The Psychoanalytic Study of the Child, 34* (1979): 349–369; L. Sander, "Infant and caretaking environment: investigation and conceptualization of adaptive behaviors in a series of increasing complexity", in E. J. Anthony (Ed.), *Explorations in Child Psychiatry* (New York: Plenum, 1975); see also B. Beebe, F. Lachmann, & J. Jaffe, "Mother–infant interaction structures and presymbolic self- and object-representations", *Psychoanalytic Dialogues, 7* (1997) (2): 133–182, and the discussions of the paper that follow in the same issue of that journal by R. Kulka, J. K. Tobin, A. Harris, and P. Fonagy.

7. See M. Klein, *The Writings of Melanie Klein, Vols. 1–4* (London: Hogarth, 1975 [reprinted London: Karnac Books, 1992–1996]); Isaacs, "The nature and function of phantasy".

8. O. F. Kernberg, *Internal World and External Reality* (New York: Jason Aronson, 1980).

9. Sandler, "Psychological conflict and the structural model".

10. M. Burgner & R. Edgcumbe, "Some problems in the conceptualization of early object relationships: Part II. The concept of object constancy", *The Psychoanalytic Study of the Child, 27* (1972): 315–333.

11. Sandler, "The background of safety".

12. Mahler, Pine, & Bergman, *The Psychological Birth of the Human Infant.*

13. Sandler, "On the concept of superego".

14. J. Sandler, "The role of affects in psychoanalytic theory", in: *From Safety to Superego* (1972/1987); see also R. Stein, *Psychoanalytic Theories of Affect* (New York: Praeger, 1991).

15. J. Sandler & W. G. Joffe, "The tendency to persistence in psychological function and development", in: *From Safety to Superego* (1967/1987).

16. J. Sandler, "Actualization and object relationships", *Journal of the Philadelphia Association for Psychoanalysis, 4* (1977): 59–70.
17. See M. Lewis & L. A. Rosenblum, *The Effect of the Infant on its Caregiver* (New York: Wiley, 1974).
18. Sandler, "Psychology and psychoanalysis"; Sandler & Rosenblatt, "The concept of the representational world".
19. Joffe & Sandler, "Adaptation, affects and the representational world".
20. Stern, *The Interpersonal World of the Infant.*
21. Sandler & Joffe, "Towards a basic psychoanalytic model".
22. S. Weinstein, "Neuropsychological studies of the phantom", in: A. L. Benton (Ed.), *Contributions to Clinical Neuropsychology* (Chicago, IL: Aldine, 1969).
23. J. Newson & E. Newson, "Intersubjectivity and the transmission of culture: on the social origins of symbolic functioning", *Bulletin of the British Psychological Society, 28* (1975): 437–446.
24. T. G. R. Bower, *Development in Infancy.* (San Francisco, CA: Freeman, 1974).
25. Newson & Newson, "Intersubjectivity and the transmission of culture".
26. See H. R. Schaffer, *The Growth of Sociability* (Harmondsworth: Penguin, 1971); "Behavioural synchrony in infancy", *New Scientist, 62* (1974): 16; see also W. S. Condon & L. W. Sander, "Neonate movement is synchronized with adult speech", *Science (N.Y.), 183* (1974): 99–101.
27. Newson & Newson, "Intersubjectivity and the transmission of culture".
28. See Sandler, "The role of affects in psychoanalytic theory".
29. Mahler, Pine, & Bergman, *The Psychological Birth of the Human Infant.*
30. Sandler (Ed.), *Projection, Identification, Projective Identification.*
31. See J. Sandler, & A.-M. Sandler, "The 'second censorship', the 'three-box model' and some technical implications", *International Journal of Psycho-Analysis, 64* (1983): 413–415; "The past unconscious, the present unconscious and the vicissitudes of guilt", *International Journal of Psycho-Analysis, 68* (1987): 331–341; "The past unconscious and the present unconscious: a contribution to a technical frame of reference", *Psychoanalytic Study of the Child, 49* (1994): 278–292.

Chapter 5

1. H. Nunberg, *Principles of Psychoanalysis: Their Application to the Neuroses* (New York: International Universities Press, 1956).
2. L. E. Hinsie & R. J. Campbell, *Psychiatric Dictionary* (fourth edition) (New York: Oxford University Press, 1940/1970).

3. S. Freud, "Character and anal erotism", in: *Standard Edition, 9* (London: Hogarth, 1908b/1953–74).

4. W. Reich, *Character-Analysis* (New York: Orgone Press, 1933/1945).

5. O. Fenichel, *The Psychoanalytic Theory of Neurosis* (New York: Norton, 1945).

6. Laplanche, J. & Pontalis, J.-B. *The Language of Psycho-Analysis* (New York: Norton, 1967/1973 [reprinted London: Karnac Books, 1996]).

7. J. Sandler, A. Holder, M. Kawenoka, H. E. Kennedy, & L. Neurath, "Notes on some theoretical and clinical aspects of transference", *International Journal of Psycho-Analysis, 50* (1969): 633–645.

8. J. A. Arlow, "Unconscious fantasy and disturbances of conscious experience", *Psychoanalytic Quarterly, 38* (1969): 1–27; "Fantasy, memory, and reality testing", *Psychoanalytic Quarterly, 38* (1969): 28–51.

9. E. Weiss, "Presenza psichica e super-io contributo all'esplorazione psicologica della coscienza morale", in *Saggi di Psicoanalisi in Onore di Sigmund Freud* (Rome: Cremonese Libraio Editore, 1936); "The psychic presence", *Bulletin of the Menninger Clinic, 3* (1939): 177–183.

Chapter 6

1. R. A. Spitz, "Anxiety in infancy: a study of its manifestation in the first year of life", *International Journal of Psycho-Analysis, 31* (1950): 138–143; Spitz, *The First Year of Life.*

2. R. A. Spitz, "Life and the dialogue", in: H. S. Gaskill (Ed.), *Counterpoint* (International Universities Press, 1963); "The derailment of dialogue: stimulus overload, action cycles and the complementary gradient", *Journal of the American Psychoanalytic Association, 12* (1964): 752–775; "The evolution of the dialogue" in: M. Schur (Ed.), *Drives, Affects, Behavior, Vol. 2* (New York: International Universities Press, 1965).

3. R. A. Spitz & M. Wolf, "The smiling response", *Genetic Psychology Monographs, 34* (1946): 57–125; Spitz, "Anxiety in infancy"; *The First Year of Life.*

4. Stern, *The Interpersonal World of the Infant;* Stern, *The Motherhood Constellation.*

5. Spitz & Wolf, "The smiling response"; Spitz, *The First Year of Life;* see also Stern, *The Motherhood Constellation.*

6. T. B. Brazelton, E. Tronick, L. Adamson, H. Als, & S. Weise, "Early mother–child reciprocity", in: *Parent–Infant Interaction* (Ciba Foundation Symposium 33, New Series) (Amsterdam: Elsevier, Excerpta Medica, 1975).

7. Spitz, *A Genetic Field Theory of Ego Formation.*

8. T. G. Decarie, *The Infant's Reaction to Strangers* (New York: International Universities Press, 1974).
9. Spitz, *The First Year of Life*.
10. J. D. Benjamin, "Further comments on some developmental aspects of anxiety", in Gaskill, *Counterpoint*.
11. L. Festinger, *A Theory of Cognitive Dissonance* (Evanston, IL: Row, Peterson, 1957).
12. K. Goldstein, *Brain Injuries in War* (London: Heinemann, 1942).
13. Sandler, "The background of safety".
14. Goldstein, *Brain Injuries in War*.
15. Mahler, Pine, & Bergman, *The Psychological Birth of the Human Infant*.
16. D. W. Winnicott, "On transference", *International Journal of Psycho-Analysis*, 37 (1956): 386–388.
17. H. Deutsch, "Some forms of emotional disturbance and their relationship to schizophrenia", *Psychoanalytic Quarterly*, 11 (1942): 301–321.
18. Goldstein, *Brain Injuries in War*.

Chapter 7

1. J. Sandler, "Reflections on some relations between psychoanalytic concepts and psychoanalytic practice", *International Journal of Psycho-Analysis*, 64 (1983): 35–46.
2. Sandler & Rosenblatt, "The concept of the representational world".
3. M. Klein, "Notes on some schizoid mechanisms", *International Journal of Psycho-Analysis*, 27 (1946): 99–110; see also Sandler (Ed.), *Projection, Identification, Projective Identification*.
4. Klein, "Notes on some schizoid mechanisms".
5. W. R. Bion, *Experiences in Groups* (London: Tavistock, 1962); *Elements of Psycho-Analysis* (London: Heinemann, 1963).
6. L. Grinberg, D. Sor, & E. D. de Bianchedi, *Introduction to the Work of Bion* (New York: Jason Aronson, 1967).
7. E. A. Ticho, "Termination of analysis: treatment goals, life goals", *Psychoanalytic Quarterly*, 41 (1972): 315–333; see also J. Sandler, & A. U. Dreher, *What Do Psychoanalysts Want? The Problem of Aims in Psychoanalytic Therapy* (London & New York: Routledge, 1996).
8. Sandler & Dreher, *What Do Psychoanalysts Want?*

Chapter 8

1. M. Klein, "The early development of conscience in the child", in: M. Klein, *Love, Guilt and Reparation and Other Works, 1921–1945* (London: Hogarth Press, 1933/1975 [reprinted London: Karnac Books, 1992]).

2. See W. T. Davison, "Panel on 'Current concepts of adult psychic structure'", *Journal of the American Psychoanalytic Association, 37* (1989): 187–198.

3. M. M. Gill, *Topography and Systems in Psychoanalytic Theory* (New York: International Universities Press, 1963).

4. Sandler & Joffe, "The tendency to persistence in psychological function and development".

5. E. Glover, "Examination of the Kleinian system of child psychology", *The Psychoanalytic Study of the Child, 9* (1945): 75–118.

6. Sandler, "On the concept of superego"; Sandler & Rosenblatt, "The concept of the representational world".

7. Sandler, "On the concept of superego".

8. Sandler, " Psychology and psychoanalysis".

9. Klein, "Notes on some schizoid mechanisms".

10. H. Hartmann, "Comments on the psychoanalytic theory of the ego", *The Psychoanalytic Study of the Child, 5* (1950): 74–96.

11. E. Jacobson, "The self and the object world: vicissitudes of their infantile cathexes and their influence on ideational and affective development", *The Psychoanalytic Study of the Child, 9* (1954): 75–127.

12. Sandler, "Reflections on some relations between psychoanalytic concepts and psychoanalytic practice".

13. Jacobson, "The self and the object world"; E. Jacobson, *The Self and the Object World* (New York: International Universities Press, 1964); Sandler, "On the concept of superego"; Sandler & Rosenblatt, "The concept of the representational world".

14. J. A. Arlow, "Object concepts and object choice", *Psychoanalytic Quarterly, 49* (1980): 109–133.

15. H. Head, *Aphasia and Kindred Disorders of Speech* (New York: Macmillan, 1926).

16. P. Schilder, *The Image and Appearance of the Human Body* (London: Routledge & Kegan Paul, 1935).

17. Sandler, " Psychology and psychoanalysis".

18. Sandler & Rosenblatt, "The concept of the representational world".

19. Sandler, "On the concept of superego"; R. Schafer, "The loving and beloved superego in Freud's structural theory", *The Psychoanalytic Study of the Child, 15* (1960): 163–188.

20. Sandler & Nagera, "The metapsychology of fantasy".

21. Sandler (Ed.), *Projection, Identification, Projective Identification*.

22. Sandler & Rosenblatt, "The concept of the representational world".

23. Sandler & Joffe, "Towards a basic psychoanalytic model".

24. See J. Sandler, & A.-M. Sandler, "A psychoanalytic theory of repression and the unconscious", in J. Sandler & P. Fonagy (Eds.), *Recovered Memories of Abuse: True or False?* (London: Karnac Books, 1997; Madison, CT: International Universities Press).

25. Freud, "Formulations on the two principles of mental functioning".
26. See Sandler & Sandler, "A psychoanalytic view of repression and the unconscious".
27. Sandler & Nagera, "The metapsychology of fantasy".
28. Freud, *The Interpretation of Dreams*; Freud, "The unconscious".
29. H. Hartmann, *Ego Psychology and the Problem of Adaptation* (London: Imago, 1939/1958); H. Hartmann, "Notes on the theory of sublimation", *The Psychoanalytic Study of the Child*, 10 (1955): 9–29.
30. Sandler & Sandler, "A psychoanalytic view of repression and the unconscious".
31. R. W. D. Fairbairn, "On the nature and aims of psychoanalytical treatment", *International Journal of Psycho-Analysis*, 39 (1958): 374–385.

BIBLIOGRAPHY

Anthony, E. J. (Ed.) (1975). *Explorations in Child Psychiatry*. New York: Plenum.

Arlow, J. A. (1969a). Unconscious fantasy and disturbances of conscious experience. *Psychoanalytic Quarterly, 38*: 1–27.

Arlow, J. A. (1969b). Fantasy, memory, and reality testing. *Psychoanalytic Quarterly, 38*: 28–51.

Arlow, J. A. (1980). Object concepts and object choice. *Psychoanalytic Quarterly, 49*: 109–133.

Beebe, B., Lachmann, F., & Jaffe, J. (1997). Mother–infant interaction structures and presymbolic self- and object-representations. *Psychoanalytic Dialogues, 7* (2): 133–182.

Benjamin, J. D. (1963). Further comments on some developmental aspects of anxiety. In: H. S. Gaskill (Ed.), *Counterpoint*. New York: International Universities Press.

Benton, A. L. (Ed.) (1969). *Contributions to Clinical Neuropsychology*. Chicago: Aldine.

Bion, W. R. (1962). *Experiences in Groups*. London: Tavistock.

Bion, W. R. (1963). *Elements of Psycho-Analysis*. London: Heinemann [reprinted London: Karnac Books, 1989].

Bower, T. G. R. (1974). *Development in Infancy*. San Francisco: Freeman.

Bowlby, J. (1969). *Attachment and Loss, Vol. 1. Attachment*. London: Hogarth Press.

Bowlby, J. (1973). *Attachment and Loss, Vol. 2. Separation, Anxiety and Anger*. London: Hogarth Press.

Brazelton, T. B., & Als, H. (1979). Four early stages in the development of mother–child interaction. *The Psychoanalytic Study of the Child, 34*: 349–369.

Brazelton, T. B., Tronick, E., Adamson, L., Als, H., & Weise, S. (1975). *Parent–Infant Interaction* (Ciba Foundation Symposium 33, New Series). Amsterdam: Elsevier, Excerpta Medica.

Burgner, M., & Edgcumbe, R. (1972). Some problems in the conceptualization of early object relationships: Part II. The concept of object constancy. *The Psychoanalytic Study of the Child, 27*: 315–333. [Reprinted London: Karnac Books, 1989.]

Condon, W. S., & Sander, L. W. (1974). Neonate movement is synchronized with adult speech. *Science (N.Y.), 183*: 99–101.

Cooper, A., Kernberg, O. F., & Person, E. (Eds.) (1989). *Psychoanalysis: Toward the Second Century*. New Haven, CT: Yale University Press.

Davison, W. T. (1989). Panel on "Current concepts of adult psychic structure". *Journal of the American Psychoanalytic Association, 37*: 187–198.

Decarie, T. G. (1974). *The Infant's Reaction to Strangers*. New York: International Universities Press.

Deutsch, H. (1942). Some forms of emotional disturbance and their relationship to schizophrenia. *Psychoanalytic Quarterly, 11*: 301–321.

Emde, R. N. (1988). Development terminable and interminable. I. Innate and motivational factors from infancy. *International Journal of Psycho-Analysis, 69*: 23–42.

Fairbairn, R. W. D. (1958). On the nature and aims of psychoanalytical treatment. *International Journal of Psycho-Analysis, 39*: 374–385.

Fenichel, O. (1945). *The Psychoanalytic Theory of Neurosis*. New York: Norton.

Festinger, L. (1957). *A Theory of Cognitive Dissonance*. Evanston, IL: Row, Peterson.

Freud, A. (1936). *The Ego and the Mechanisms of Defence*. London: Hogarth [reprinted London: Karnac Books, 1993].

Freud, S. (1894a). The neuro-psychoses of defence. *Standard Edition, 3*.

Freud, S. (1895d) (with J. Breuer). *Studies on Hysteria. Standard Edition, 2*.

Freud, S. (1896b). Further remarks on the neuro-psychoses of defence. *Standard Edition, 3*.

Freud, S. (1897–1902). *The Origins of Psycho-Analysis: Letters to Wilhelm Fliess, Drafts and Notes*. London: Imago, 1954.

Freud, S. (1900a). *The Interpretation of Dreams. Standard Edition, 4–5*.

Freud, S. (1905e [1901]). Fragment of an analysis of a case of hysteria. *Standard Edition, 7*.

Freud, S. (1908b). Character and anal erotism. *Standard Edition, 9*.

Freud, S. (1911b). Formulations on the two principles of mental functioning. *Standard Edition, 12*.

Freud, S. (1914c). On narcissism: an introduction. *Standard Edition, 14*.

Freud, S. (1915e). The unconscious. *Standard Edition, 14*.

Freud, S. (1920g). *Beyond the Pleasure Principle. Standard Edition, 18*.

Freud, S. (1923b). *The Ego and the Id. Standard Edition, 19*.

Freud, S. (1926d [1925]). *Inhibitions, Symptoms and Anxiety. Standard Edition, 20*.

Freud, S. (1940a [1938]). *An Outline of Psycho-Analysis. Standard Edition, 23*.

Gaskill, H. S. (Ed.) (1963). *Counterpoint*. New York: International Universities Press.

Gill, M. M. (1963). *Topography and Systems in Psychoanalytic Theory*. New York: International Universities Press.

Glover, E. (1945). Examination of the Klein system of child psychology. *The Psychoanalytic Study of the Child, 9*: 75–118.

Goldstein, K. (1942). *Brain Injuries in War*. London: Heinemann.

Grinberg, L., Sor, D., & de Bianchedi, E. D. (1967). *Introduction to the Work of Bion*. New York: Jason Aronson.

Hartmann, H. (1939). *Ego Psychology and the Problem of Adaptation*. London: Imago, 1958.

Hartmann, H. (1950). Comments on the psychoanalytic theory of the ego. *The Psychoanalytic Study of the Child, 5*: 74–96.

Hartmann, H. (1955). Notes on the theory of sublimation. *The Psychoanalytic Study of the Child, 10*: 9–29.

Head, H. (1926). *Aphasia and Kindred Disorders of Speech*. New York: Macmillan.

Heimann, P. (1950). On counter-transference. *International Journal of Psycho-Analysis, 31*: 81–4.

Heimann, P. (1960). Counter-transference. *British Journal of Medical Psychology, 33*: 9–15.

Hinsie, L. E., & Campbell, R. J. (1940). *Psychiatric Dictionary* (fourth edition). New York: Oxford University Press, 1970.

Isaacs, S. (1948). The nature and function of phantasy. *International Journal of Psycho-Analysis, 29*: 73–97.

Jacobson, E. (1954). The self and the object world: vicissitudes of their infantile cathexes and their influence on ideational and affective development. *The Psychoanalytic Study of the Child, 9*: 75–127.

Jacobson, E. (1964). *The Self and the Object World.* New York: International Universities Press.

Kernberg, O. F. (1976). *Object Relations Theory and Clinical Psychoanalysis.* New York: Jason Aronson.

Kernberg, O. F. (1980). *Internal World and External Reality.* New York: Jason Aronson.

Kernberg, O. F. (1982). Self, ego, affects and drives. *Journal of the American Psychoanalytic Association, 30*: 893–917.

King, P., & Steiner, R. (Eds.) (1991). *The Freud–Klein Controversies 1941–1945.* London: Routledge.

Klein, M. (1933). The early development of conscience in the child. In: M. Klein, *Love, Guilt and Reparation and Other Works, 1921–1945.* London: Hogarth Press, 1975 [reprinted London: Karnac Books, 1992].

Klein, M. (1946). Notes on some schizoid mechanisms. *International Journal of Psycho-Analysis, 27*: 99–110.

Klein, M. (1975a). *Love, Guilt and Reparation and Other Works, 1921–1945.* London: Hogarth Press [reprinted London: Karnac Books, 1992].

Klein, M. (1975b). *The Writings of Melanie Klein, Vols. 1–4.* London: Hogarth [reprinted London: Karnac Books, 1992–96].

Kris, E. (1947). Problems in clinical research: discussion remarks. *American Journal of Orthopsychiatry, 17*: 210–214.

Laplanche, J., & Pontalis, J.-B. (1967). *The Language of Psycho-Analysis.* New York: Norton, 1973 [reprinted London: Karnac Books, 1996].

Lewis, M., & Rosenblum, L. A. (1974). *The Effect of the Infant on Its Caregiver.* New York: Wiley.

Mahler, M. S., Pine, F., & Bergman, A. (1975). *The Psychological Birth of the Human Infant.* New York: Basic Books [reprinted London: Karnac Books, 1991].

Newson, J., & Newson, E. (1975). Intersubjectivity and the transmission of culture: on the social origins of symbolic functioning. *Bulletin of the British Psychological Society, 28*: 437–446.

Nunberg, H. (1956). *Principles of Psychoanalysis: Their Application to the Neuroses.* New York: International Universities Press.

Reich, W. (1933). *Character-Analysis.* New York: Orgone Press, 1945.

Rexford, E. N., Sander, L. W., & Shapiro, T. (Eds.) (1976). *Infant Psychiatry.* New Haven, CT: Yale University Press.

Sander, L. (1975). Infant and caretaking environment: investigation and conceptualization of adaptive behaviors in a series of increasing complexity. In: E. J. Anthony (Ed.), *Explorations in Child Psychiatry.* New York: Plenum.

Sandler, A.-M. (1975). Comments on the significance of Piaget's work for psychoanalysis. *International Review of Psycho-Analysis, 2*: 365–378.

Sandler, A.-M. (1977). Beyond eight-month anxiety. *International Journal of Psycho-Analysis, 58*: 195–208.

Sandler, J. (1959). On the repetition of early childhood relationships in later psychosomatic illness. In: *The Nature of Stress Disorder*, Proceedings of a Conference of the Society for Psychosomatic Research. London: Hutchinson.

Sandler, J. (1970). Sexual phantasies and sexual theories in childhood. In: *Studies on Child Psychoanalysis: Pure and Applied.* New Haven, CT: Yale University Press.

Sandler, J. (1974). Psychological conflict and the structural model: some clinical and theoretical implications. *International Journal of Psycho-Analysis, 55*: 53–62.

Sandler, J. (1976a). Countertransference and role-responsiveness. *International Review of Psycho-Analysis, 3*: 43–47.

Sandler, J. (1976b). Dreams, unconscious phantasies and "identity of perception". *International Review of Psycho-Analysis, 3*: 33–42.

Sandler, J. (1977). Actualization and object relationships. *Journal of the Philadelphia Association for Psychoanalysis, 4*: 59–70.

Sandler, J. (1981). Character traits and object relationships. *Psychoanalytic Quarterly, 50*: 694–708.

Sandler, J. (1983). Reflections on some relations between psychoanalytic concepts and psychoanalytic practice. *International Journal of Psycho-Analysis, 64*: 35–46.

Sandler, J. (Ed.) (1987a). *Projection, Identification, Projective Identification.* New York: International Universities Press; London: Karnac Books.

Sandler, J. (Ed.) (1987b). *From Safety to Superego.* New York: Guilford Press; London: Karnac Books.

Sandler, J. (Ed.) (1989). *Dimensions of Psychoanalysis*. London: Karnac Books; Madison CT: International Universities Press.

Sandler, J. (1990a). Internal objects and internal object relationships. *Psychoanalytic Inquiry, 10*: 163–181.

Sandler, J. (1990b). On internal object relations. *Journal of the American Psychoanalytic Association, 38*: 859–880.

Sandler, J. (1992). Reflections on developments in the theory of psychoanalytic technique. *International Journal of Psycho-Analysis, 73*: 189–198.

Sandler, J. (1996). Comments on the psychodynamics of interaction. *Psychoanalytic Inquiry, 16*: 88–95.

Sandler, J., Dare, C., & Holder, A. (1973). *The Patient and the Analyst*. London: Karnac Books; New York: International Universities Press. [Revised edition London: Karnac Books, 1992].

Sandler, J., & Dreher, A. U. (1996). *What Do Psychoanalysts Want? The Problem of Aims in Psychoanalytic Therapy*. London & New York: Routledge.

Sandler, J., & Fonagy, P. (Eds.) (1997). *Recovered Memories of Abuse: True or False?* London: Karnac Books; Madison, CT: International Universities Press.

Sandler, J., with A. Freud (1985). *The Analysis of Defense*. New York: International Universities Press.

Sandler, J., Holder, A., Dare, C., & Dreher, A. U. (1997). *Freud's Models of the Mind: An Introduction*. London: Karnac Books; Madison CT: International Universities Press.

Sandler, J., Holder, A., Kawenoka, M., Kennedy, H. E., & Neurath, L. (1969). Notes on some theoretical and clinical aspects of transference. *International Journal of Psycho-Analysis, 50*: 633–645.

Sandler, J., & Joffe, W. G. (1965). Notes on childhood depression. *International Journal of Psycho-Analysis, 46*: 88–96.

Sandler, J., Kawenoka, M., Neurath, L., Rosenblatt, B., Schnurmann, A., & Sigal, J. (1962). The classification of superego material in the Hampstead Index. *The Psychoanalytic Study of the Child, 17*: 107–127.

Sandler, J., & Sandler, A.-M. (1978). On the development of object relationships and affects. *International Journal of Psycho-Analysis, 59*: 285–296.

Sandler, J., & Sandler, A.-M. (1983). The "second censorship", the "three-box model" and some technical implications. *International Journal of Psycho-Analysis, 64*: 413–415.

Sandler, J., & Sandler, A.-M. (1987). The past unconscious, the present unconscious and the vicissitudes of guilt. *International Journal of Psycho-Analysis, 68*: 331–341.

Sandler, J., & Sandler, A.-M. (1994). The past unconscious and the present unconscious: a contribution to a technical frame of reference. *Psychoanalytic Study of the Child, 49*: 278–292.

Schafer, R. (1960). The loving and beloved superego in Freud's structural theory. *The Psychoanalytic Study of the Child, 15*: 163–188.

Schaffer, H. R. (1971). *The Growth of Sociability*. Harmondsworth: Penguin.

Schaffer, H. R. (1974). Behavioural synchrony in infancy. *New Scientist, 62*: 16.

Schilder, P. (1935). *The Image and Appearance of the Human Body*. London: Routledge & Kegan Paul.

Schur, M. (Ed.) (1965). *Drives, Affects, Behavior, Vol. 2*. New York: International Universities Press.

Schur, M. (1966). *The Id and the Regulatory Principles of Mental Functioning*. New York: International Universities Press.

Spitz, R. A. (1950). Anxiety in infancy: a study of its manifestation in the first year of life. *International Journal of Psycho-Analysis, 31*: 138–143.

Spitz, R. A. (1959). *A Genetic Field Theory of Ego Formation*. New York: International Universities Press.

Spitz, R. A. (1963). Life and the dialogue. In: H. S. Gaskill (Ed.), *Counterpoint*. New York: International Universities Press.

Spitz, R. A. (1964). The derailment of dialogue: stimulus overload, action cycles and the complementary gradient. *Journal of the American Psychoanalytic Association, 12*: 752–775.

Spitz, R. A. (1965a). The evolution of the dialogue. In: M. Schur (Ed.), *Drives, Affects, Behavior, Vol. 2*. New York: International Universities Press.

Spitz, R. A. (1965b). *The First Year of Life*. New York: International Universities Press.

Spitz, R. A., & Wolf, M. (1946). The smiling response. *Genetic Psychology Monographs, 34*: 57–125.

Stein, R. (1991). *Psychoanalytic Theories of Affect*. New York: Praeger.

Stern, D. N. (1985). *The Interpersonal World of the Infant*. New York: Basic Books [reprinted London: Karnac Books, 1998].

Stern, D. N. (1995). *The Motherhood Constellation*. New York: Basic Books [reprinted London: Karnac Books, 1998].

Stone, L. J., Smith, H. T., & Murphy, L. B. (Eds.) (1974). *The Competent Infant*. London: Tavistock.

Ticho, E. A. (1972). Termination of analysis: treatment goals, life goals. *Psychoanalytic Quarterly, 41*: 315–333.

Wangh, M. (1962). The "evocation of a proxy": a psychological maneuver, its use as a defense, its purposes and genesis. *The Psychoanalytic Study of the Child, 17*: 451–469.

Weinstein, S. (1969). Neuropsychological studies of the phantom. In: A. L. Benton (Ed.), *Contributions to Clinical Neuropsychology*. Chicago: Aldine.

Weiss, E. (1936). *Saggi di Psicoanalisi in Onore di Sigmund Freud*. Rome: Cremonese Libraio Editore.

Weiss, E. (1939). The psychic presence. *Bulletin of the Menninger Clinic, 3*: 177–183.

Winnicott, D. W. (1953). Transitional objects and transitional phenomena. *International Journal of Psycho-Analysis, 34*: 89–97. [In: *Playing and Reality*. London: Tavistock, 1971.]

Winnicott, D. W. (1956). On transference. *International Journal of Psycho-Analysis, 37*: 386–388.

Winnicott, D. W. (1960a). Countertransference. *British Journal of Medical Psychology, 33*: 17–21. [In: *The Maturational Processes and the Facilitating Environment*. London: Hogarth, 1965; reprinted London: Karnac Books, 1990.]

Winnicott, D. W. (1960b). The theory of the parent–infant relationship. *International Journal of Psycho-Analysis, 41*: 585–595. [In: *The Maturational Processes and the Facilitating Environment*. London: Hogarth, 1965; reprinted London: Karnac Books, 1990.]

Winnicott, D. W. (1971). *Playing and Reality*. London: Tavistock.

INDEX

Abraham, K., 123
acting out, 35
actualization, xvii–xix, 4, 27, 41–44,
    65, 86, 117, 129, 135, 140
  through daydreams, 42, 66
  definition of term, 41
  delusional, 42, 66
  forms of, 42
  hallucinatory, 42, 66
  through illusional perception, 42,
    66
  through modification, 66
  role of, 132–133
  and role-responsiveness, 47–56
  symbolic, 42, 66
  and wish-fulfilment, 42, 65, 66,
    77, 83, 129
actual self ("self-of-the-moment"),
  12
Adamson, L., 147
adaptation:
  motives for, 21
  theory of, 17

affect(s):
  defence against, vs. defence
    against instinct, 21
  vs. drive, 22
  and object relations, 57–77
  role of, in self–object interaction,
    19
  as subjective experiences, xx
affective state(s):
  conscious/unconscious, change
    in, 31, 60
  pain as, 14
  of well-being, 10, 11, 14, 15
    restoration of, 75
affirmation, need for, 19–20, 61
aggression, child's, 75
aggressive affects, xx
aggressive drive(s), xvi, xx, 9
aggressor, identification with, 134
A-group (Klein Group) of British
    Psycho-Analytical Society,
    ix
Als, H., 145, 147